STATUTORY INSTRUMENTS

1986 No. 1915 (S. 139)

INSOLVENCY

COMPANIES

The Insolvency (Scotland) Rules 1986

Made - - - -	10*th November* 1986
Laid before Parliament	26*th November* 1986
Coming into Operation	29*th December* 1986

ARRANGEMENT OF THE RULES

INTRODUCTORY PROVISIONS

PART 1

COMPANY VOLUNTARY ARRANGEMENTS

CHAPTER 1

PRELIMINARY

CHAPTER 2

PROPOSAL BY DIRECTORS

CHAPTER 3

PROPOSAL BY ADMINISTRATOR OR LIQUIDATOR WHERE HE IS THE NOMINEE

CHAPTER 4

PROPOSAL BY ADMINISTRATOR OR LIQUIDATOR WHERE ANOTHER INSOLVENCY PRACTITIONER IS THE NOMINEE

CHAPTER 5

MEETINGS

CHAPTER 6

IMPLEMENTATION OF THE VOLUNTARY ARRANGEMENT

PART 2

ADMINISTRATION PROCEDURE

CHAPTER 1

APPLICATION FOR, AND MAKING OF, THE ORDER

CHAPTER 2

STATEMENT OF AFFAIRS AND PROPOSALS TO CREDITORS

CHAPTER 3

MEETINGS AND NOTICES

CHAPTER 4

THE CREDITORS' COMMITTEE

CHAPTER 5

THE ADMINISTRATOR

CHAPTER 6

VAT BAD DEBT RELIEF

PART 3

RECEIVERS

CHAPTER 1

APPOINTMENT

3.1.   Acceptance of appointment.

CHAPTER 2

STATEMENT OF AFFAIRS

3.2.   Notice requiring statement of affairs.
3.3.   Expenses of statement of affairs.

CHAPTER 3

THE CREDITORS' COMMITTEE

3.4.   Constitution of committee.
3.5.   Functions of the committee.
3.6.   Application of provisions relating to liquidation committee.
3.7.   Information from receiver.
3.8.   Members' dealings with the company.

CHAPTER 4

MISCELLANEOUS

3.9.   Abstract of receipts and payments.
3.10.   Receiver deceased.
3.11.   Vacation of office.

CHAPTER 5

VAT BAD DEBT RELIEF

3.12.   Issue of certificate of insolvency.
3.13.   Notice to creditors.
3.14.   Preservation of certificate with company's records.

PART 4

WINDING UP BY THE COURT

CHAPTER 1

PROVISIONAL LIQUIDATOR

CHAPTER 2

STATEMENT OF AFFAIRS

CHAPTER 3

INFORMATION

CHAPTER 4

MEETINGS OF CREDITORS AND CONTRIBUTORIES

CHAPTER 5

CLAIMS IN LIQUIDATION

CHAPTER 6

THE LIQUIDATOR

SECTION A: APPOINTMENT AND FUNCTIONS OF LIQUIDATOR

SECTION B: REMOVAL AND RESIGNATION; VACATION OF OFFICE

SECTION C: RELEASE ON COMPLETION OF WINDING UP

SECTION D: OUTLAYS AND REMUNERATION

SECTION E: SUPPLEMENTARY PROVISIONS

CHAPTER 7

THE LIQUIDATION COMMITTEE

CHAPTER 8

THE LIQUIDATION COMMITTEE WHERE WINDING UP FOLLOWS IMMEDIATELY ON ADMINISTRATION

CHAPTER 9

DISTRIBUTION OF COMPANY'S ASSETS BY LIQUIDATOR

CHAPTER 10

SPECIAL MANAGER

CHAPTER 11

PUBLIC EXAMINATION OF COMPANY OFFICERS AND OTHERS

CHAPTER 12

MISCELLANEOUS

CHAPTER 13

COMPANY WITH PROHIBITED NAME

PART 5

CREDITORS' VOLUNTARY WINDING UP

PART 6

MEMBERS' VOLUNTARY WINDING UP

PART 7

PROVISIONS OF GENERAL APPLICATION

CHAPTER 1

MEETINGS

CHAPTER 2

PROXIES AND COMPANY REPRESENTATION

CHAPTER 3

MISCELLANEOUS

SCHEDULE 1   Rule 5

Modifications of Part 4 in relation to creditors' voluntary winding up.

SCHEDULE 2   Rule 6

Application of Part 4 in relation to members' voluntary winding up.

SCHEDULE 3   Rule 7.4(6)

Deposit Protection Board's voting rights.

SCHEDULE 4   Rule 7.29

Punishment of Offences under the Rules.

SCHEDULE 5   Rule 7.30

Index of Forms

Part 1:	*Company voluntary arrangements*
Form 1.1 (Scot)	Notice of report of a meeting approving voluntary arrangement.
Form 1.2 (Scot)	Notice of order of revocation or suspension of voluntary arrangement.
Form 1.3 (Scot)	Notice of voluntary arrangement supervisor's abstract of receipts and payments.
Form 1.4 (Scot)	Notice of completion of voluntary arrangement.
Part 2:	*Administration Procedure*
Form 2.1 (Scot)	Notice of petition for administration order.
Form 2.2 (Scot)	Notice of administration order.
Form 2.3 (Scot)	Notice of dismissal of petition for administration order.
Form 2.4 (Scot)	Notice of discharge of administration order.
Form 2.5 (Scot)	Notice requiring submission of administration statement of affairs.
Form 2.6 (Scot)	Statement of affairs.
Form 2.7 (Scot)	Notice of statement of administrator's proposals.
Form 2.8 (Scot)	Notice of result of meeting of creditors.

11

Form 4.24 (Scot)	Notice of certificate that creditors have been paid in full.
Form 4.25 (Scot)	Declaration of solvency.
Form 4.26 (Scot)	Return of final meeting in a voluntary winding up.
Form 4.27 (Scot)	Notice of court's order sisting proceedings in winding up by the Court.
Form 4.28 (Scot)	Notice under section 204(6) or 205(6).

The Secretary of State, in exercise of the powers conferred on him by section 411 of the Insolvency Act 1986(a) and of all other powers enabling him in that behalf, hereby makes the following Rules:-

INTRODUCTORY PROVISIONS

Citation and commencement

0.1. These Rules may be cited as the Insolvency (Scotland) Rules 1986 and shall come into operation on 29th December 1986.

Interpretation

0.2.—(1) In these Rules

"the Act" means the Insolvency Act 1986;

"the Companies Act" means the Companies Act 1985(b);

"the Bankruptcy Act" means the Bankruptcy (Scotland) Act 1985(c);

"the Rules" means the Insolvency (Scotland) Rules 1986;

"accounting period" in relation to the winding up of a company, shall be construed in accordance with section 52(1) and (6) of the Bankruptcy Act as applied by Rule 4.68;

"business day" means any day other than a Saturday, a Sunday, Christmas Day, Good Friday or a day which is a bank holiday in any part of Great Britain;

"company" means a company which the courts in Scotland have jurisdiction to wind up;

"insolvency proceedings" means any proceedings under the first group of Parts in the Act or under these Rules;

"receiver" means a receiver appointed under section 51 (Receivers (Scotland)); and

"responsible insolvency practitioner" means, in relation to any insolvency proceedings, the person acting as supervisor of a voluntary arrangement under Part I of the Act, or as administrator, receiver, liquidator or provisional liquidator.

(2) In these Rules, unless the context otherwise requires, any reference -

(a) to a section is a reference to a section of the Act;

(b) to a Rule is a reference to a Rule of the Rules;

(c) to a Part or a Schedule is a reference to a Part of, or Schedule to, the Rules;

(d) to a Chapter is a reference to a Chapter of the Part in which that reference is made.

Application

0.3. These Rules apply -

(a) 1986 c.45.
(b) 1985 c.6.
(c) 1985 c.66.

(a) to receivers appointed, and

(b) to all other insolvency proceedings which are commenced, on or after the date on which the Rules come into operation.

PART I

COMPANY VOLUNTARY ARRANGEMENTS

CHAPTER 1

PRELIMINARY

Scope of this Part; interpretation

1.1.—(1) The Rules in this Part apply where, pursuant to Part I of the Act, it is intended to make and there is made a proposal to a company and to its creditors for a voluntary arrangement, that is to say, a composition in satisfaction of its debts or a scheme of arrangement of its affairs.

(2) In this Part -

(a) Chapter 2 applies where the proposal for a voluntary arrangement is made by the directors of the company, and neither is the company in liquidation nor is an administration order under Part II of the Act in force in relation to it;

(b) Chapter 3 applies where the company is in liquidation or an administration order is in force and the proposal is made by the liquidator or (as the case may be) the administrator, he in either case being the nominee for the purposes of the proposal;

(c) Chapter 4 applies in the same case as Chapter 3, but where the nominee is an insolvency practitioner other than the liquidator or administrator; and

(d) Chapters 5 and 6 apply in all of the three cases mentioned in sub-paragraphs *(a)* to *(c)* above.

(3) In Chapters 3, 4 and 5 the liquidator or the administrator is referred to as the "responsible insolvency practitioner".

CHAPTER 2

PROPOSAL BY DIRECTORS

Preparation of proposal

1.2. The directors shall prepare for the intended nominee a proposal on which (with or without amendments to be made under Rule 1.3 below) to make his report to the court under section 2.

Contents of proposal

1.3.—(1) The directors' proposal shall provide a short explanation why, in their opinion, a voluntary arrangement under Part I of the Act is desirable, and give reasons why the company's creditors may be expected to concur with such an arrangement.

(2) The following matters shall be stated, or otherwise dealt with, in the directors' proposal -

(a) the following matters, so far as within the directors' immediate knowledge -

(i) the company's assets, with an estimate of their respective values;

(ii) the extent (if any) to which the assets are subject to any security in favour of any creditors;

(iii) the extent (if any) to which particular assets of the company are to be excluded from the voluntary arrangement;

(b) particulars of any property other than assets of the company itself, which is proposed to be included in the arrangement, the source of such property and the terms on which it is to be made available for inclusion;

(c) the nature and amount of the company's liabilities (so far as within the directors' immediate knowledge), the manner in which they are proposed to be met, modified, postponed or otherwise dealt with by means of the arrangement, and (in particular) -

(i) how it is proposed to deal with preferential creditors (defined in section 386) and creditors who are, or claim to be, secured;

(ii) how persons connected with the company (being creditors) are proposed to be treated under the arrangement; and

(iii) whether there are, to the directors' knowledge, any circumstances giving rise to the possibility, in the event that the company should go into liquidation, of claims under -

section 242 (gratuitous alienations),

section 243 (unfair preferences),

section 244 (extortionate credit transactions), or

section 245 (floating charges invalid);

and, where any such circumstances are present, whether, and if so how, it is proposed under the voluntary arrangement to make provision for wholly or partly indemnifying the company in respect of such claims;

(d) whether any, and if so what, cautionary obligations (including guarantees) have been given of the company's debts by other persons, specifying which (if any) of the cautioners are persons connected with the company;

(e) the proposed duration of the voluntary arrangement;

(f) the proposed dates of distributions to creditors, with estimates of their amounts;

(g) the amount proposed to be paid to the nominee (as such) by way of remuneration and expenses;

(h) the manner in which it is proposed that the supervisor of the arrangement should be remunerated and his expenses defrayed;

(i) whether, for the purposes of the arrangement, any cautionary obligations (including guarantees) are to be offered by directors, or other persons, and whether (if so) any security is to be given or sought;

(j) the manner in which funds held for the purposes of the arrangement are to be banked, invested or otherwise dealt with pending distribution to creditors;

(k) the manner in which funds held for the purpose of payment to creditors, and not so paid on the termination of the arrangement, are to be dealt with;

(*l*) the manner in which the business of the company is being and is proposed to be conducted during the course of the arrangement;

(*m*) details of any further credit facilities which it is intended to arrange for the company and how the debts so arising are to be paid;

(*n*) the functions which are to be undertaken by the supervisor of the arrangement;

(*o*) the name, address and qualification of the person proposed as supervisor of the voluntary arrangement, and confirmation that he is (so far as the directors are aware) qualified to act as an insolvency practitioner in relation to the company.

(3) With the agreement in writing of the nominee, the directors' proposal may be amended at any time up to delivery of the former's report to the court under section 2(2).

Notice to intended nominee

1.4.—(1) The directors shall give to the intended nominee written notice of their proposal.

(2) The notice, accompanied by a copy of the proposal, shall be delivered either to the nominee himself, or to a person authorised to take delivery of documents on his behalf.

(3) If the intended nominee agrees to act, he shall cause a copy of the notice to be endorsed to the effect that it has been received by him on a specified date; and the period of 28 days referred to in section 2(2) then runs from that date.

(4) The copy of the notice so endorsed shall be returned by the nominee forthwith to the directors at an address specified by them in the notice for that purpose.

Statement of affairs

1.5.—(1) The directors shall,within 7 days after their proposal is delivered to the nominee, or within such longer time as he may allow, deliver to him a statement of the company's affairs.

(2) The statement shall comprise the following particulars (supplementing or amplifying, so far as is necessary for clarifying the state of the company's affairs, those already given in the directors' proposal):-

(*a*) a list of the company's assets, divided into such categories as are appropriate for easy identification, with estimated values assigned to each category;

(*b*) in the case of any property on which a claim against the company is wholly or partly secured, particulars of the claim and its amount and of how and when the security was created;

(*c*) the names and addresses of the company's preferential creditors (defined in section 386), with the amounts of their respective claims;

(*d*) the names and addresses of the company's unsecured creditors, with the amounts of their respective claims;

(e) particulars of any debts owed by or to the company to or by persons connected with it;

(f) the names and addresses of the company's members and details of their respective shareholdings; and

(g) such other particulars (if any) as the nominee may in writing require to be furnished for the purposes of making his report to the court on the directors' proposal.

(3) The statement of affairs shall be made up to a date not earlier than 2 weeks before the date of the notice given by the directors to the nominee under Rule 1.4. However the nominee may allow an extension of that period to the nearest practicable date (not earlier than 2 months before the date of the notice under Rule 1.4); and if he does so, he shall give his reasons in his report to the court on the directors' proposal.

(4) The statement shall be certified as correct, to the best of their knowledge and belief, by two or more directors of the company or by the company secretary and at least one director (other than the secretary himself).

Additional disclosure for assistance of nominee

1.6.—(1) If it appears to the nominee that he cannot properly prepare his report on the basis of information in the directors' proposal and statement of affairs, he may call on the directors to provide him with -

(a) further and better particulars as to the circumstances in which, and the reasons why, the company is insolvent or (as the case may be) threatened with insolvency;

(b) particulars of any previous proposals which have been made in respect of the company under Part I of the Act;

(c) any further information with respect to the company's affairs which the nominee thinks necessary for the purposes of his report.

(2) The nominee may call on the directors to inform him, with respect to any person who is, or at any time in the 2 years preceding the notice under Rule 1.4 has been, a director or officer of the company, whether and in what circumstances (in those 2 years or previously) that person -

(a) has been concerned in the affairs of any other company (whether or not incorporated in Scotland) which has become insolvent, or

(b) has had his estate sequestrated, granted a trust deed for his creditors, been adjudged bankrupt or compounded or entered into an arrangement with his creditors.

(3) For the purpose of enabling the nominee to consider their proposal and prepare his report on it, the directors must give him access to the company's accounts and records.

Nominee's report on the proposal

1.7.—(1) With his report to the court under section 2 the nominee shall lodge -

(a) a copy of the directors' proposal (with amendments, if any, authorised under Rule 1.3(3));

(b) a copy or summary of the company's statement of affairs.

(2) If the nominee makes known his opinion that meetings of the company and its creditors should be summoned under section 3, his report shall have annexed to it his comments on the proposal. If his opinion is otherwise, he shall give his reasons for that opinion.

(3) The nominee shall send a copy of his report and of his comments (if any) to the company. Any director, member or creditor of the company is entitled, at all reasonable times on any business day, to inspect the report and comments.

Replacement of nominee

1.8. Where any person intends to apply to the court under section 2(4) for the nominee to be replaced he shall give to the nominee at least 7 days' notice of his application.

Summoning of meetings under section 3

1.9.—(1) If in his report the nominee states that in his opinion meetings of the company and its creditors should be summoned to consider the directors' proposal, the date on which the meetings are to be held shall be not less than 14, nor more than 28 days from the date on which he lodged his report in court under section 2.

(2) The notice summoning the meeting shall specify the court in which the nominee's report under section 2 has been lodged and with each notice there shall be sent -

(a) a copy of the directors' proposal;

(b) a copy of the statement of affairs or, if the nominee thinks fit, a summary of it (the summary to include a list of creditors and the amount of their debts); and

(c) the nominee's comments on the proposal.

CHAPTER 3

PROPOSAL BY ADMINISTRATOR OR LIQUIDATOR WHERE HE IS THE NOMINEE

Preparation of proposal

1.10. The responsible insolvency practitioner's proposal shall specify -

(a) all such matters as under Rule 1.3 in Chapter 2 the directors of the company would be required to include in a proposal by them, and

(b) such other matters (if any) as the insolvency practitioner considers appropriate for ensuring that members and creditors of the company are enabled to reach an informed decision on the proposal.

Summoning of meetings under section 3

1.11.—(1) The responsible insolvency practitioner shall give at least 14 days' notice of the meetings of the company and of its creditors under section 3(2).

(2) With each notice summoning the meeting, there shall be sent -

(a) a copy of the responsible insolvency practitioner's proposal; and

(b) a copy of the company's statement of affairs or, if he thinks fit, a summary of it (the summary to include a list of the creditors and the amount of their debts).

CHAPTER 4

PROPOSAL BY ADMINISTRATOR OR LIQUIDATOR WHERE ANOTHER INSOLVENCY PRACTITIONER IS THE NOMINEE

Preparation of proposal and notice to nominee

1.12.—(1) The responsible insolvency practitioner shall give notice to the intended nominee, and prepare his proposal for a voluntary arrangement, in the same manner as is required of the directors in the case of a proposal by them, under Chapter 2.

(2) Rule 1.2 applies to the responsible insolvency practitioner as it applies to the directors; and Rule 1.4 applies as regards the action to be taken by the nominee.

(3) The content of the proposal shall be as required by Rule 1.3, reading references to the directors as referring to the responsible insolvency practitioner.

(4) Rule 1.6 applies, in respect of the information to be provided to the nominee, reading references to the directors as referring to the responsible insolvency practitioner.

(5) With the proposal the responsible insolvency practitioner shall provide a copy of the company's statement of affairs.

(6) Rules 1.7 to 1.9 apply as regards a proposal under this Chapter as they apply to a proposal under Chapter 2.

CHAPTER 5

MEETINGS

General

1.13. The provisions of Chapter 1 of Part 7 (Meetings) shall apply with regard to the meetings of the company and of the creditors which are summoned under section 3, subject to Rules 1.9, 1.11 and 1.12(6) and the provisions in this Chapter.

Summoning of meetings

1.14.—(1) In fixing the date, time and place for the creditors' meeting and the company meeting, the person summoning the meetings ("the convenor") shall have regard primarily to the convenience of the creditors.

(2) The meetings shall be held on the same day and in the same place, but the creditors' meeting shall be fixed for a time in advance of the company meeting.

Attendance by company officers

1.15.—(1) At least 14 days' notice to attend the meetings shall be given by the convenor to -

(a) all directors of the company, and

(b) any persons in whose case the convenor thinks that their presence is required as being officers of the company or as having been directors or officers of it at any time in the 2 years immediately preceding the date of the notice.

(2) The chairman may, if he thinks fit, exclude any present or former director or officer from attendance at a meeting, either completely or for any part of it; and this applies whether or not a notice under this Rule has been sent to the person excluded.

Adjournments

1.16.—(1) On the day on which the meetings are held, they may from time to time be adjourned; and, if the chairman thinks fit for the purpose of obtaining the simultaneous agreement of the meetings to the proposal (with the same modifications, if any), the meetings may be held together.

(2) If on that day the requisite majority for the approval of the voluntary arrangement (with the same modifications, if any) has not been obtained from both creditors and members of the company, the chairman may, and shall, if it is so resolved, adjourn the meetings for not more than 14 days.

(3) If there are subsequently further adjournments, the final adjournment shall not be to a day later than 14 days after the date on which the meetings were originally held.

(4) There shall be no adjournment of either meeting unless the other is also adjourned to the same business day.

(5) In the case of a proposal by the directors, if the meetings are adjourned under paragraph (2), notice of the fact shall be given by the nominee forthwith to the court.

(6) If following any final adjournment of the meetings the proposal (with the same modifications, if any) is not agreed by both meetings, it is deemed rejected.

Report of meetings

1.17.—(1) A report of the meetings shall be prepared by the person who was chairman of them.

(2) The report shall -

(a) state whether the proposal for a voluntary arrangement was approved or rejected and, if approved, with what (if any) modifications;

(b) set out the resolutions which were taken at each meeting, and the decision on each one;

(c) list the creditors and members of the company (with their respective values) who were present or represented at the meeting, and how they voted on each resolution; and *(d)* include such further information (if any) as the chairman thinks it appropriate to make known to the court.

(3) A copy of the chairman's report shall, within 4 days of the meetings being held, be lodged in court.

(4) In respect of each of the meetings the persons to whom notice of the result of the meetings is to be sent under section 4(6) are all those who were sent notice of the meeting. The notice shall be sent immediately after a copy of the chairman's report is lodged in court under paragraph (3).

(5) If the voluntary arrangement has been approved by the meetings (whether or not in the form proposed) the chairman shall forthwith send a copy of the report to the registrar of companies. *Form 1.1 (Scot)*

CHAPTER 6

IMPLEMENTATION OF THE VOLUNTARY ARRANGEMENT

Resolutions to follow approval

1.18.—(1) If the voluntary arrangement is approved (with or without modifications) by the two meetings, a resolution may be taken by the creditors, where two or more insolvency practitioners are appointed to act as supervisor, on the question whether acts to be done in connection with the arrangement may be done by one of them or are to be done by both or all.

(2) A resolution under paragraph (1) may be passed in anticipation of the approval of the voluntary arrangement by the company meeting if such meeting has not at that time been concluded.

(3) If at either meeting a resolution is moved for the appointment of some person other than the nominee to be supervisor of the arrangement, there must be produced to the chairman, at or before the meeting -

(a) that person's written consent to act (unless the person is present and then and there signifies his consent), and

(b) his written confirmation that he is qualified to act as an insolvency practitioner in relation to the company.

Hand-over of property, etc. to supervisor

1.19.—(1) After the approval of the voluntary arrangement, the directors or, where -

(a) the company is in liquidation or is subject to an administration order, and

(b) a person other than the responsible insolvency practitioner is appointed as supervisor of the voluntary arrangement,

the responsible insolvency practitioner, shall forthwith do all that is required for putting the supervisor into possession of the assets included in the arrangement.

(2) Where paragraph (1)*(a)* and *(b)* applies, the supervisor shall, on taking possession of the assets, discharge any balance due to the responsible insolvency practitioner by way of remuneration or on account of -

(a) fees, costs, charges and expenses properly incurred and payable under the Act or the Rules, and

(b) any advances made in respect of the company, together with interest on such advances at the official rate (within the meaning of Rule 4.66(2)(*b*)) ruling at the date on which the company went into liquidation or (as the case may be) became subject to the administration order.

(3) Alternatively, the supervisor shall, before taking possession, give the responsible insolvency practitioner a written undertaking to discharge any such balance out of the first realisation of assets.

(4) The sums due to the responsible insolvency practitioner as above shall be paid out of the assets included in the arrangement in priority to all other sums payable out of those assets, subject only to the deduction from realisations by the supervisor of the proper costs and expenses of such realisations.

(5) The supervisor shall from time to time out of the realisation of assets discharge all cautionary obligations (including guarantees) properly given by the responsible insolvency practitioner for the benefit of the company and shall pay all the responsible insolvency practitioner's expenses.

Revocation or suspension of the arrangement

1.20.—(1) This Rule applies where the court makes an order of revocation or suspension under section 6.

(2) The person who applied for the order shall serve copies of it -

(a) on the supervisor of the voluntary arrangement, and

(b) on the directors of the company or the administrator or liquidator (according to who made the proposal for the arrangement).

Service on the directors may be effected by service of a single copy of the order on the company at its registered office.

(3) If the order includes a direction given by the court, under section 6(4)(*b*), for any further meetings to be summoned, notice shall also be given by the person who applied for the order to whoever is, in accordance with the direction, required to summon the meetings.

(4) The directors or (as the case may be) the administrator or liquidator shall -

(a) forthwith after receiving a copy of the court's order, give notice of it to all persons who were sent notice of the creditors' and the company meetings or who, not having been sent that notice, appear to be affected by the order; and

(b) within 7 days of their receiving a copy of the order (or within such longer period as the court may allow), give notice to the court whether it is intended to make a revised proposal to the company and its creditors, or to invite re-consideration of the original proposal.

(5) The person on whose application the order of revocation or suspension was made shall, within 7 days after the making of the order, deliver a copy of the order to the registrar of companies.

Form 1.2
(Scot)

Supervisor's accounts and reports

1.21.—(1) Where the voluntary arrangement authorises or requires the supervisor -

(a) to carry on the business of the company, or to trade on its behalf or in its name, or

(b) to realise assets of the company, or

(c) otherwise to administer or dispose of any of its funds,

he shall keep accounts and records of his acts and dealings in and in connection with the arrangement, including in particular records of all receipts and payments of money.

(2) The supervisor shall, not less often than once in every 12 months beginning with the date of his appointment, prepare an abstract of such receipts and payments and send copies of it, accompanied by his comments on the progress and efficacy of the arrangement, to -

(a) the court,

(b) the registrar of companies,   *Form 1.3 (Scot)*

(c) the company,

(d) all those of the company's creditors who are bound by the arrangement,

(e) subject to paragraph (5) below, the members of the company who are so bound, and

(f) where the company is not in liquidation, the company's auditors for the time being.

If in any period of 12 months he has made no payments and had no receipts, he shall at the end of that period send a statement to that effect to all those specified in sub-paragraphs (a) to (f) above.

(3) An abstract provided under paragraph (2) shall relate to a period beginning with the date of the supervisor's appointment or (as the case may be) the day following the end of the last period for which an abstract was prepared under this Rule; and copies of the abstract shall be sent out, as required by paragraph (2), within the two months following the end of the period to which the abstract relates.

(4) If the supervisor is not authorised as mentioned in paragraph (1), he shall, not less often than once in every 12 months beginning with the date of his appointment, send to all those specified in paragraphs 2(a) to (f) a report on the progress and efficacy of the voluntary arrangement.

(5) The court may, on application by the supervisor, -

(a) dispense with the sending under this Rule of abstracts or reports to members of the company, either altogether or on the basis that the availability of the abstract or report to members on request is to be advertised by the supervisor in a specified manner;

(b) vary the dates on which the obligation to send abstracts or reports arises.

Fees, costs, charges and expenses

1.22. The fees, costs, charges and expenses that may be incurred for any of the purposes of a voluntary arrangement are -

24

(a) any disbursements made by the nominee prior to the approval of the arrangement, and any remuneration for his services as is agreed between himself and the company (or, as the case may be, the administrator or liquidator);

(b) any fees, costs, charges or expenses which -

    (i) are sanctioned by the terms of the arrangement, or

    (ii) would be payable, or correspond to those which would be payable, in an administration or winding up.

Completion of the arrangement

1.23.—(1) Not more than 28 days after the final completion of the voluntary arrangement, the supervisor shall send to all creditors and members of the company who are bound by it a notice that the voluntary arrangement has been fully implemented.

(2) With the notice there shall be sent to each creditor and member a copy of a report by the supervisor, summarising all receipts and payments made by him in pursuance of the arrangement, and explaining any difference in the actual implementation of it as compared with the proposal approved by the creditors' and company meetings.

(3) The supervisor shall, within the 28 days mentioned above, send to the registrar of companies and to the court a copy of the notice to creditors and *Form 1.4* *(Scot)* members under paragraph (1), together with a copy of the report under paragraph (2).

(4) The court may, on application by the supervisor, extend the period of 28 days under paragraphs (1) or (3).

False representations, etc.

1.24.—(1) A person being a past or present officer of a company commits an offence if he make any false representation or commits any other fraud for the purpose of obtaining the approval of the company's members or creditors to a proposal for a voluntary arrangement under Part I of the Act.

(2) For this purpose "officer" includes a shadow director.

(3) A person guilty of an offence under this Rule is liable to imprisonment or a fine, or both.

PART 2

ADMINISTRATION PROCEDURE

CHAPTER 1

APPLICATION FOR, AND MAKING OF, THE ORDER

Independent report on company's affairs

2.1.—(1) Where it is proposed to apply to the court by way of petition for an administration order to be made under section 8 in relation to a company, there may be prepared in support of the petition a report by an independent person to the effect that the appointment of an administrator for the company is expedient.

(2) The report may be by the person proposed as administrator, or by any other person having adequate knowledge of the company's affairs, not being a director, secretary, manager, member or employee of the company.

(3) The report shall specify which of the purposes specified in section 8(3) may, in the opinion of the person preparing it, be achieved for the company by the making of an administration order in relation to it.

Notice of petition

2.2.—(1) Under section 9(2)(*a*), notice of the petition shall forthwith be given *Form 2.1 (Scot)* by the petitioner to the person who has appointed, or is or may be entitled to appoint, an administrative receiver, and to the following persons:-

(*a*) an administrative receiver, if appointed;

(*b*) if a petition for the winding up of the company has been presented but no order for winding up has yet been made, the petitioner under that petition;

(*c*) a provisional liquidator, if appointed;

(*d*) the person proposed in the petition to be the administrator;

(*e*) the registrar of companies;

(*f*) the Keeper of the Register of Inhibitions and Adjudications for recording in that register; and

(*g*) the company, if the petition for the making of an administration order is presented by the directors or by a creditor or creditors of the company.

(2) Notice of the petition shall also be given to the persons upon whom the court orders that the petition be served.

Notice and advertisement of administration order

2.3.—(1) If the court makes an administration order, it shall forthwith give notice of the order to the person appointed as administrator.

(2) Under section 21(1)(*a*) the administrator shall forthwith after the order is made, advertise the making of the order once in the Edinburgh Gazette and once in a newspaper circulating in the area where the company has its principal place of business or in such newspaper as he thinks most appropriate for ensuring that the order comes to the notice of the company's creditors.

26

(3) Under section 21(2), the administrator shall send a notice with a copy of *Form 2.2 (Scot)* the court's order certified by the clerk of court to the registrar of companies, and in addition shall send a copy of the order to the following persons:-

>   *(a)* any person who has appointed an administrative receiver, or has power to do so;
>
>   *(b)* an administrative receiver, if appointed;
>
>   *(c)* a petitioner in a petition for the winding up of the company, if that petition is pending;
>
>   *(d)* any provisional liquidator of the company, if appointed; and
>
>   *(e)* the Keeper of the Register of Inhibitions and Adjudications for recording in that register.

(4) If the court dismisses the petition under section 9(4) or discharges the administration order under section 18(3) or 24(5), the petitioner or, as the case may be, the administrator shall -

>   *(a)* forthwith send a copy of the court's order dismissing the petition or *Form 2.3 (Scot)* effecting the discharge to the Keeper of the Register of Inhibitions and *Form 2.4 (Scot)* Adjudications for recording in that register; and
>
>   *(b)* within 14 days after the date of making of the order, send a notice with *Form 2.3 (Scot)* a copy, certified by the clerk of court, of the court's order dismissing the *Form 2.4 (Scot)* petition or effecting the discharge to the registrar of companies.

(5) Paragraph (4) is without prejudice to any order of the court as to the persons by and to whom, and how, notice of any order made by the court under section 9(4), 18 or 24 is to be given and to section 18(4) or 24(6) (notice by administrator of court's order discharging administration order).

CHAPTER 2

STATEMENT OF AFFAIRS AND PROPOSALS TO CREDITORS

Notice requiring statement of affairs

2.4.—(1) This Rule and Rules 2.5 and 2.6 apply where the administrator decides to require a statement as to the affairs of the company to be made out and submitted to him in accordance with section 22.

(2) The administrator shall send to each of the persons upon whom he decides to make such a requirement under section 22, a notice in the form required by Rule 7.30 and Schedule 5 requiring him to make out and submit a statement *Form 2.5 (Scot)* of affairs.

(3) Any person to whom a notice is sent under this Rule is referred to in this Chapter as "a deponent".

Form of the statement of affairs

2.5.—(1) The statement of affairs shall be in the form required by Rule 7.30 *Form 2.6 (Scot)* and Schedule 5.

(2) The administrator shall insert any statement of affairs submitted to him in the sederunt book.

Expenses of statement of affairs

2.6.—(1) A deponent who makes up and submits to the administrator a statement of affairs shall be allowed and be paid by the administrator out of his receipts, any expenses incurred by the deponent in so doing which the administrator considers to be reasonable.

(2) Any decision by the administrator under this Rule is subject to appeal to the court.

(3) Nothing in this Rule relieves a deponent from any obligation to make up and submit a statement of affairs, or to provide information to the administrator.

Statement to be annexed to proposals

2.7. There shall be annexed to the administrator's proposals, when sent to the registrar of companies under section 23 and laid before the creditors' meeting to be summoned under that section, a statement by him showing - *Form 2.7 (Scot)*

(a) details relating to his appointment as administrator, the purposes for which an administration order was applied for and made, and any subsequent variation of those purposes;

(b) the names of the directors and secretary of the company;

(c) an account of the circumstances giving rise to the application for an administration order;

(d) if a statement of affairs has been submitted, a copy or summary of it with the administrator's comments, if any;

(e) if no statement of affairs has been submitted, details of the financial position of the company at the latest practicable date (which must, unless the court otherwise orders, be a date not earlier than that of the administration order);

(f) the manner in which the affairs of the company will be managed and its business financed, if the administrator's proposals are approved; and

(g) such other information (if any) as the administrator thinks necessary to enable creditors to decide whether or not to vote for the adoption of the proposals.

Notices of proposals to members

2.8. Any notice required to be published by the administrator -

(a) under section 23(2)(b) (notice of address for members of the company to write for a copy of the administrator's statement of proposals), and

(b) under section 25(3)(b) (notice of address for members of the company to write for a copy of the administrator's statement of proposed revisions to the proposals),

shall be inserted once in the Edinburgh Gazette and once in the newspaper in which the administrator's appointment was advertised.

CHAPTER 3

MEETINGS AND NOTICES

General

2.9. The provisions of Chapter 1 of Part 7 (Meetings) shall apply with regard to meetings of the company's creditors or members which are summoned by the administrator, subject to the provisions in this Chapter.

Meeting to consider administrator's proposals

2.10.—(1) The administrator shall give at least 14 days' notice to attend the meeting of the creditors under section 23(1) to any directors or officers of the company (including persons who have been directors or officers in the past) whose presence at the meeting is, in the administrator's opinion, required.

(2) If at the meeting there is not the requisite majority for approval of the administrator's proposals (with modifications, if any), the chairman may, and shall if a resolution is passed to that effect, adjourn the meeting for not more than 14 days.

Retention of title creditors

2.11. For the purpose of entitlement to vote at a creditors' meeting in administration proceedings, a seller of goods to the company under a retention of title agreement shall deduct from his claim the value, as estimated by him, of any rights arising under that agreement in respect of goods in the possession of the company.

Hire-purchase, conditional sale and hiring agreements

2.12.—(1) Subject as follows, an owner of goods under a hire-purchase agreement or under an agreement for the hire of goods for more than 3 months, or a seller of goods under a conditional sale agreement, is entitled to vote in respect of the amount of the debt due and payable to him by the company as at the date of the administration order.

(2) In calculating the amount of any debt for this purpose, no account shall be taken of any amount attributable to the exercise of any right under the relevant agreement, so far as the right has become exercisable solely by virtue of the presentation of the petition for an administration order or any matter arising in consequence of that or of the making of the order.

Report of meetings

2.13. Any report by the administrator of the proceedings of creditors' meetings held under section 23(1) or 25(2) shall have annexed to it details of the proposals which were considered by the meeting in question and of any modifications which were also considered.

Notices to creditors

2.14.—(1) Within 14 days after the conclusion of a meeting of creditors to consider the administrator's proposals or proposed revisions under section 23(1) or 25(2), the administrator shall send notice of the result of the meeting (including, where appropriate, details of the proposals as approved) to every creditor to whom notice of the meeting was sent and to any other creditor of whom the administrator has become aware since the notice was sent.

(2) Within 14 days after the end of every period of 6 months beginning with the date of approval of the administrator's proposals or proposed revisions, the administrator shall send to all creditors of the company a report on the progress of the administration.

(3) On vacating office, the administrator shall send to creditors a report on the administration up to that time. This does not apply where the administration is immediately followed by the company going into liquidation, nor where the administrator is removed from office by the court or ceases to be qualified to act as an insolvency practitioner.

CHAPTER 4

THE CREDITORS' COMMITTEE

Application of provisions in Part 3 (Receivers)

2.15.—(1) Chapter 3 of Part 3 (The creditors' committee) shall apply with regard to the creditors' committee in the administration as it applies to the creditors' committee in receivership, subject to the modifications specified below and to any other necessary modifications. *Form 4.20 (Scot) Form 4.22 (Scot)*

(2) For any reference in the said Chapter 3, or in any provision of Chapter 7 of Part 4 as applied by Rule 3.6, to the receiver, receivership or the creditors' committee in receivership, there shall be substituted a reference to the administrator, the administration and the creditors' committee in the administration.

(3) In Rule 3.4(1) and 3.7(1), for the reference to section 68 or 68(2), there shall be substituted a reference to section 26 or 26(2).

(4) For Rule 3.5 there shall be substituted the following Rule:-

"Functions of the Committee

3.5. The creditors' committee shall assist the administrator in discharging his functions and shall act in relation to him in such manner as may be agreed from time to time.".

CHAPTER 5

THE ADMINISTRATOR

Remuneration

2.16.—(1) The administrator's remuneration shall be determined from time to time by the creditors' committee or, if there is no creditors' committee, by the court, and shall be paid out of the assets as an expense of the administration.

(2) The basis for determining the amount of the remuneration payable to the administrator may be a commission calculated by reference to the value of the company's property with which he has to deal, but there shall in any event be taken into account -

(a) the work which, having regard to that value, was reasonably undertaken by him; and

(b) the extent of his responsibilities in administering the company's assets.

(3) Rules 4.32 to 4.34 of Chapter 6 of Part 4 shall apply to an administration as they apply to a liquidation but as if for any reference to the liquidator or the liquidation committee there was substituted a reference to the administrator or the creditors committee.

Abstract of receipts and payments

2.17.—(1) The administrator shall - *Form 2.9*
(Scot)

(a) within 2 months after the end of 6 months from the date of his appointment, and of every subsequent period of 6 months, and

(b) within 2 months after he ceases to act as administrator,

send to the court, and to the registrar of companies, and to each member of the creditors' committee, the requisite accounts of the receipts and payments of the company.

(2) The court may, on the administrator's application, extend the period of 2 months mentioned in paragraph (1).

(3) The accounts are to be in the form of an abstract showing - *Form 2.9*
(Scot)

(a) receipts and payments during the relevant period of 6 months, or

(b) where the administrator has ceased to act, receipts and payments during the period from the end of the last 6 month period to the time when he so ceased (alternatively, if there has been no previous abstract, receipts and payments in the period since his appointment as administrator).

(4) If the administrator makes default in complying with this Rule, he is liable to a fine and, for continued contravention, to a daily default fine.

Resignation from office

2.18.—(1) The administrator may give notice of his resignation on grounds *Form 2.13*
(Scot) of ill health or because -

(a) he intends ceasing to be in practice as an insolvency practitioner, or

(b) there is some conflict of interest or change of personal circumstances, which precludes or makes impracticable the further discharge by him of the duties of administrator.

(2) The administrator may, with the leave of the court, give notice of his resignation on grounds other than those specified in paragraph (1).

(3) The administrator must give to the persons specified below at least 7 days' notice of his intention to resign, or to apply for the court's leave to do so -

(a) if there is a continuing administrator of the company, to him;

(b) if there is no such administrator, to the creditors' committee; and

(c) if there is no such administrator and no creditors' committee, to the company and its creditors.

Administrator deceased

2.19.—(1) Subject to the following paragraph, where the administrator has died, it is the duty of his executors or, where the deceased administrator was a partner in a firm, of a partner of that firm to give notice of that fact to the court, specifying the date of the death. This does not apply if notice has been given under the following paragraph.

(2) Notice of the death may also be given by any person producing to the court a copy of the death certificate.

Order filling vacancy

2.20. Where the court makes an order filling a vacancy in the office of administrator, the same provisions apply in respect of giving notice of, and advertising, the appointment as in the case of the original appointment of an administrator.

CHAPTER 6

VAT BAD DEBT RELIEF

Application of provisions in Part 3 (Receivers)

2.21. Chapter 5 of Part 3 (VAT bad debt relief) shall apply to an administrator as it applies to an administrative receiver, subject to the modification that, for any reference to the administrative receiver, there shall be substituted a reference to the administrator.

PART 3

RECEIVERS

CHAPTER 1

APPOINTMENT

Acceptance of Appointment

3.1.—(1) Where a person has been appointed a receiver by the holder of a floating charge under section 53, his acceptance (which need not be in writing) of that appointment for the purposes of paragraph *(a)* of section 53(6) shall be intimated by him to the holder of the floating charge or his agent within the period specified in that paragraph and he shall, as soon as possible after his acceptance, endorse a written docquet to that effect on the instrument of appointment.

(2) The written docquet evidencing receipt of the instrument of appointment, which is required by section 53(6)*(b)*, shall also be endorsed on the instrument of appointment.

(3) The receiver shall, as soon as possible after his acceptance of the appointment, deliver a copy of the endorsed instrument of appointment to the holder of the floating charge or his agent.

(4) This Rule shall apply in the case of the appointment of joint receivers as it applies to the appointment of a receiver, except that, where the docquet of acceptance required by paragraph (1) is endorsed by each of the joint receivers, or two or more of them, on the same instrument of appointment, it is the joint receiver who last endorses his docquet of acceptance who is required to send a copy of the instrument of appointment to the holder of the floating charge or his agent under paragraph (3).

CHAPTER 2

STATEMENT OF AFFAIRS

Notice requiring statement of affairs

3.2.—(1) Where the receiver decides to require from any person or persons a statement as to the affairs of the company to be made out and submitted to him in accordance with section 66, he shall send to each of those persons a notice in the form required by Rule 7.30 and Schedule 5 requiring him to make out *Form 3.1 (Scot)* and submit a statement of affairs in the form prescribed by the Receivers (Scotland) Regulations 1986(**a**).

(2) Any person to whom a notice is sent under this Rule is referred to in this Chapter as "a deponent".

(3) The receiver shall insert any statement of affairs submitted to him in the sederunt book.

(**a**) S.I 1986/1917.

Expenses of statement of affairs

3.3.—(1) A deponent who makes up and submits to the receiver a statement of affairs shall be allowed and be paid by the receiver, as an expense of the receivership, any expenses incurred by the deponent in so doing which the receiver considers to be reasonable.

(2) Any decision by the receiver under this Rule is subject to appeal to the court.

(3) Nothing in this Rule relieves a deponent from any obligation to make up and submit a statement of affairs, or to provide information to the receiver.

CHAPTER 3

THE CREDITORS' COMMITTEE

Constitution of committee

3.4.—(1) Where it is resolved by the creditors' meeting to establish a creditors' committee under section 68, the committee shall consist of at least 3 and not more than 5 creditors of the company elected at the meeting.

(2) Any creditor of the company who has lodged a claim is eligible to be a member of the committee, so long as his claim has not been rejected for the purpose of his entitlement to vote.

(3) A body corporate or a partnership may be a member of the committee, but it cannot act as such otherwise than by a representative appointed under Rule 7.20, as applied by Rule 3.6.

Functions of the committee

3.5. In addition to the functions conferred on it by the Act, the creditors' committee shall represent to the receiver the views of the unsecured creditors and shall act in relation to him in such manner as may be agreed from time to time.

Application of provisions relating to liquidation committee

3.6.—(1) Chapter 7 of Part 4 (The liquidation committee) shall apply with regard to the creditors' committee in the receivership and its members as it applies to the liquidation committee and the creditor members thereof, subject to the modifications specified below and to any other necessary modifications. *Form 4.20 (Scot) Form 4.22 (Scot)*

(2) For any reference in the said Chapter 7 to -

(a) the liquidator or the liquidation committee, there shall be substituted a reference to the receiver or to the creditors' committee;

(b) to the creditor member, there shall be substituted a reference to a creditor,

and any reference to a contributory member shall be disregarded.

(3) In Rule 4.42(3) and 4.52(2), for the reference to Rule 4.41(1), there shall be substituted a reference to Rule 3.4(1).

(4) In Rule 4.57,

(a) for the reference to an expense of the liquidation, there shall be substituted a reference to an expense of the receivership;

(b) at the end of that Rule there shall be inserted the following:-

"This does not apply to any meeting of the committee held within 3 months of a previous meeting, unless the meeting in question is summoned at the instance of the receiver.".

(5) The following Rules shall not apply, namely -

Rules 4.40, 4.41, 4.43 to 4.44, 4.53, 4.56, 4.58 and 4.59.

Information from receiver

3.7.—(1) Where the committee resolves to require the attendance of the receiver under section 68(2), the notice to him shall be in writing signed by the majority of the members of the committee for the time being or their representatives.

(2) The meeting at which the receiver's attendance is required shall be fixed by the committee for a business day, and shall be held at such time and place as he determines.

(3) Where the receiver so attends, the members of the committee may elect any one of their number to be chairman of the meeting, in place of the receiver or any nominee of his.

Members' dealings with the company

3.8.—(1) Membership of the committee does not prevent a person from dealing with the company while the receiver is acting, provided that any transactions in the course of such dealings are entered into on normal commercial terms.

(2) The court may, on the application of any person interested, set aside a transaction which appears to it to be contrary to the requirements of this Rule, and may give such consequential directions as it thinks fit for compensating the company for any loss which it may have incurred in consequence of the transaction.

CHAPTER 4

MISCELLANEOUS

Abstract of receipts and payments

3.9.—(1) The receiver shall -

(a) within 2 months after the end of 12 months from the date of his appointment, and of every subsequent period of 12 months, and

(b) within 2 months after he ceases to act as receiver,

send the requisite accounts of his receipts and payments as receiver to -   *Form 3.2 (Scot)*

    (i) the registrar of companies,

    (ii) the holder of the floating charge by virtue of which he was appointed,

    (iii) the members of the creditors' committee (if any),

(iv) the company or, if it is in liquidation, the liquidator.

(2) The court may, on the receiver's application, extend the period of 2 months referred to in paragraph (1).

(3) The accounts are to be in the form of an abstract showing - *Form 3.2 (Scot)*

(a) receipts and payments during the relevant period of 12 months, or

(b) where the receiver has ceased to act, receipts and payments during the period from the end of the last 12-month period to the time when he so ceased (alternatively, if there has been no previous abstract, receipts and payments in the period since his appointment as receiver).

(4) This Rule is without prejudice to the receiver's duty to render proper accounts required otherwise than as above.

(5) If the receiver makes default in complying with this Rule, he is liable to a fine and, for continued contravention, to a daily default fine.

Receiver deceased

3.10. If the receiver dies, the holder of the floating charge by virtue of which he was appointed shall, forthwith on his becoming aware of the death, give notice of it to - *Form 3.3 (Scot)*

(a) the registrar of companies,

(b) the members of the creditors' committee (if any),

(c) the company or, if it is in liquidation, the liquidator,

(d) the holder of any other floating charge and any receiver appointed by him.

Vacation of office

3.11. The receiver, on vacating office on completion of the receivership or in consequence of his ceasing to be qualified as an insolvency practitioner, shall, in addition to giving notice to the registrar of companies under section 62(5), give notice of his vacating office, within 14 days thereof, to -

(a) the holder of the floating charge by virtue of which he was appointed,

(b) the members of the creditors' committee (if any),

(c) the company or, if it is in liquidation, the liquidator,

(d) the holder of any other floating charge and any receiver appointed by him.

CHAPTER 5

VAT BAD DEBT RELIEF

Issue of certificate of insolvency

3.12.—(1) In accordance with this Rule, it is the duty of the administrative receiver to issue a certificate in the terms of paragraph *(b)* of section 22(3) of the Value Added Tax Act 1983(**a**) (which specifies the circumstances in which a company is deemed insolvent for the purposes of that section) forthwith upon his forming the opinion described in that paragraph.

(**a**) 1983 c.55, as amended by section 32 of the Finance Act 1985 c.54.

(2) There shall in the certificate be specified -

(a) the name of the company and its registered number;

(b) the name of the administrative receiver and the date of his appointment; and

(c) the date on which the certificate is issued.

(3) The certificate shall be entitled "CERTIFICATE OF INSOLVENCY FOR THE PURPOSES OF SECTION 22(3)*(b)* OF THE VALUE ADDED TAX ACT 1983".

Notice to creditors

3.13.—(1) Notice of the issue of the certificate shall be given by the administrative receiver within 3 months of his appointment or within 2 months of issuing the certificate, whichever is the later, to all of the company's unsecured creditors of whose address he is then aware and who have, to his knowledge, made supplies to the company, with a charge to value added tax, at any time before his appointment.

(2) Thereafter, he shall give the notice to any such creditor of whose address and supplies to the company he becomes aware.

(3) He is not under obligation to provide any creditor with a copy of the certificate.

Preservation of certificate with company's records

3.14.—(1) The certificate shall be retained with the company's accounting records, and section 222 of the Companies Act (where and for how long records are to be kept) shall apply to the certificate as it applies to those records.

(2) It is the duty of the administrative receiver, on vacating office, to bring this Rule to the attention of the directors or (as the case may be) any successor of his as receiver.

PART 4

WINDING UP BY THE COURT

CHAPTER 1

PROVISIONAL LIQUIDATOR

Appointment of provisional liquidator

4.1. An application to the court for the appointment of a provisional liquidator under section 135 may be made by the petitioner in the winding up, or by a creditor of the company, or by a contributory, or by the company itself, or by any person who under any enactment would be entitled to present a petition for the winding up of the company.

Order of appointment

4.2 (1) The provisional liquidator shall forthwith after the order appointing him is made, give notice of his appointment to -

Form 4.9 (Scot)

(a) the registrar of companies;

(b) the company; and

(c) any receiver of the whole or any part of the property of the company.

(2) The provisional liquidator shall advertise his appointment in accordance with any directions of the court.

Caution

4.3. The cost of providing the caution required by the provisional liquidator under the Act shall unless the court otherwise directs be -

(a) if a winding up order is not made, reimbursed to him out of the property of the company, and the court may make an order against the company accordingly, and

(b) if a winding up order is made, reimbursed to him as an expense of the liquidation.

Failure to find or to maintain caution

4.4.—(1) If the provisional liquidator fails to find or to maintain his caution, the court may remove him and make such order as it thinks fit as to expenses.

(2) If an order is made under this Rule removing the provisional liquidator, or discharging the order appointing him, the court shall give directions as to whether any, and if so what, steps should be taken for the appointment of another person in his place.

Remuneration

4.5.—(1) The remuneration of the provisional liquidator shall be fixed by the court from time to time.

(2) Section 53(4) of the Bankruptcy Act shall apply to determine the basis for fixing the amount of the remuneration of the provisional liquidator, subject to the modifications specified in Rule 4.16(2) and to any other necessary modifications.

(3) The provisional liquidator's remuneration shall, unless the court otherwise directs, be paid to him, and the amount of any expenses incurred by him reimbursed -

(a) if a winding up order is not made, out of the property of the company (and the court may make an order against the company accordingly), and

(b) if a winding up order is made, as an expense of the liquidation.

Termination of appointment

4.6.—(1) The appointment of the provisional liquidator may be terminated by the court on his application, or on that of any of the persons entitled to make application for his appointment under Rule 4.1.

(2) If the provisional liquidator's appointment terminates, in consequence of the dismissal of the winding up petition or otherwise, the court may give such directions as it thinks fit with respect to -

(a) the accounts of his administration;

(b) the expenses properly incurred by the provisional liquidator; or

(c) any other matters which it thinks appropriate

and, without prejudice to the power of the court to make an order against any other person, may direct that any expenses properly incurred by the provisional liquidator during the period of his appointment, including any remuneration to which he is entitled, be paid out of the property of the company, and authorise him to retain out of that property such sums as are required for meeting those expenses.

CHAPTER 2

STATEMENT OF AFFAIRS

Notice requiring statement of affairs

4.7.—(1) This Chapter applies where the liquidator or, in a case where a provisional liquidator is appointed, the provisional liquidator decides to require a statement as to the affairs of the company to be made out and submitted to him in accordance with section 131.

(2) In this Chapter the expression "liquidator" includes "provisional liquidator".

(3) The liquidator shall send to each of the persons upon whom he decides to make such a requirement under section 131, a notice in the form required by Rule 7.30 and Schedule 5 requiring him to make out and submit a statement *Form 4.3 (Scot)* of affairs.

(4) Any person to whom a notice is sent under this Rule is referred to in this Chapter as "a deponent".

Form of the statement of affairs

4.8.—(1) The statement of affairs shall be in the form required by Rule 7.30 *Form 4.4 (Scot)* and Schedule 5.

(2) The liquidator shall insert any statement of affairs submitted to him in the sederunt book.

Expenses of statement of affairs

4.9.—(1) At the request of any deponent, made on the grounds that he cannot himself prepare a proper statement of affairs, the liquidator may authorise an allowance towards expenses to be incurred by the deponent in employing some person or persons to be approved by the liquidator to assist the dependent in preparing it.

(2) Any such request by the deponent shall be accompanied by an estimate of the expenses involved.

(3) An authorisation given by the liquidator under this Rule shall be subject to such conditions (if any) as he thinks fit to impose with respect to the manner in which any person may obtain access to relevant books and papers.

(4) Nothing in this Rule relieves a deponent from any obligation to make up and submit a statement of affairs, or to provide information to the liquidator.

(5) Any allowance by the liquidator under this Rule shall be an expense of the liquidation.

(6) The liquidator shall intimate to the deponent whether he grants or refuses his request for an allowance under this Rule and where such request is refused the deponent affected by the refusal may appeal to the court not later than 14 days from the date intimation of such refusal is made to him.

CHAPTER 3

INFORMATION

Information to creditors and contributories

4.10.—(1) The liquidator shall report to the creditors and, except where he considers it would be inappropriate to do so, the contributories with respect to the proceedings in the winding up within six weeks after the end of each accounting period or he may submit such a report to a meeting of creditors or of contributories held within such period.

(2) Any reference in this Rule to creditors is to persons known to the liquidator to be creditors of the company.

(3) Where a statement of affairs has been submitted to him, the liquidator may send out to creditors and contributories with the next convenient report to be made under paragraph (1) a summary of the statement and such observations (if any) as he thinks fit to make with respect to it.

Information to registrar of companies

4.11. The statement which section 192 requires the liquidator to send to the *Form 4.5 (Scot)* registrar of companies if the winding up is not concluded within one year from its commencement, shall be sent not more than 30 days after the expiration of that year and thereafter at 6 monthly intervals until the winding up is concluded *Form 4.6 (Scot)* in the form required by Rule 7.30 and Schedule 5 and shall contain the particulars specified therein.

CHAPTER 4

MEETINGS OF CREDITORS AND CONTRIBUTORIES

First meetings in the liquidation

4.12.—(1) This Rule applies where under section 138(3) the interim liquidator summons meetings of the creditors and the contributories of the company for the purpose of choosing a person to be liquidator of the company in place of the interim liquidator.

(2) Meetings summoned by the interim liquidator under that section are known respectively as "the first meeting of creditors" and "the first meeting of contributories", and jointly as "the first meetings in the liquidation".

(3) Subject as follows, no resolutions shall be taken at the first meeting of creditors other than the following:-

> *(a)* a resolution to appoint one or more named insolvency practitioners to be liquidator or, as the case may be, joint liquidators and, in the case of joint liquidators, whether any act required or authorised to be done by the liquidator is to be done by both or all of them, or by any one or more;

> *(b)* a resolution to establish a liquidation committee under section 142(1);

> *(c)* unless a liquidation committee is to be established, a resolution specifying the terms on which the liquidator is to be remunerated, or to defer consideration of that matter;

> *(d)* a resolution to adjourn the meeting for not more than 3 weeks;

> *(e)* any other resolution which the chairman considers it right to allow for special reason.

(4) This rule also applies with respect to the first meeting of contributories except that that meeting shall not pass any resolution to the effect of paragraph (3)(*c*).

Other meetings

4.13.—(1) The liquidator shall summon a meeting of the creditors in each year during which the liquidation is in force.

(2) Subject to the above provision, the liquidator may summon a meeting of the creditors or of the contributories at any time for the purpose of ascertaining their wishes in all matters relating to the liquidation.

Attendance at meetings of company's personnel

4.14.—(1) This Rule applies to meetings of creditors and to meetings of contributories.

(2) Whenever a meeting is summoned, the liquidator may, if he thinks fit, give at least 21 days' notice to any one or more of the company's personnel that he is or they are required to be present at the meeting or be in attendance.

(3) In this Rule, "the company's personnel" means the persons referred to in paragraphs *(a)* to *(d)* of section 235(3) (present and past officers, employees, etc.).

(4) The liquidator may authorise payment to any person whose attendance is requested at a meeting under this Rule of his reasonable expenses incurred in travelling to the meeting and any payment so authorised shall be an expense of the liquidation.

(5) In the case of any meeting, any of the company's personnel may, if he has given reasonable notice of his wish to be present, be admitted to take part; but this is at the discretion of the chairman of the meeting, whose decision as to what (if any) intervention may be made by any of them is final.

(6) If it is desired to put questions to any of the company's personnel who are not present, the meeting may be adjourned with a view to obtaining his attendance.

(7) Where one of the company's personnel is present at a meeting, only such questions may be put to him as the chairman may in his discretion allow.

CHAPTER 5

CLAIMS IN LIQUIDATION

Submission of claims

4.15.—(1) A creditor, in order to obtain an adjudication as to his entitlement -

(a) to vote at any meeting of the creditors in the liquidation; or

(b) to a dividend (so far as funds are available) out of the assets of the company in respect of any accounting period,

shall submit his claim to the liquidator -

(a) at or before the meeting; or, as the case may be,

(b) not later than 8 weeks before the end of the accounting period.

(2) A creditor shall submit his claim by producing to the liquidator -

(a) a statement of claim in the form required by Rule 7.30 and Schedule 5; *Form 4.7 (Scot)* and

(b) an account or voucher (according to the nature of the debt claimed) which constitutes *prima facie* evidence of the debt,

but the liquidator may dispense with any requirement of this paragraph in respect of any debt or any class of debt.

(3) A claim submitted by a creditor, which has been accepted in whole or in part by the liquidator for the purpose of voting at a meeting or of drawing a dividend in respect of any accounting period, shall be deemed to have been resubmitted for the purpose of obtaining an adjudication as to his entitlement both to vote at any subsequent meeting and (so far as funds are available) to a dividend in respect of an accounting period or, as the case may be, any subsequent accounting period.

(4) A creditor, who has submitted a claim, may at any time submit a further claim specifying a different amount for his claim:

Provided that a secured creditor shall not be entitled to produce a further claim specifying a different value for the security at any time after the liquidator has required the creditor to discharge, or convey or assign, the security under paragraph 5(2) of Schedule 1 to the Bankruptcy Act, as applied by the following Rule.

(5) Votes are calculated according to the amount of a creditor's debt as at the date of the commencement of the winding up within the meaning of section 129, deducting any amounts paid in respect of that debt after that date.

(6) In this Rule and in Rule 4.16, including the provisions of the Bankruptcy Act applied by that Rule, any reference to the liquidator includes a reference to the chairman of the meeting.

Application of the Bankruptcy Act

4.16.—(1) Subject to the provisions in this Chapter, the following provisions of the Bankruptcy Act shall apply in relation to a liquidation of a company in like manner as they apply in a sequestration of a debtor's estate, subject to the modifications specified in paragraph (2) and to any other necessary modifications:-

(a) section 22(5) and (10) (criminal offence in relation to producing false claims or evidence);

(b) section 48(5), (6) and (8), together with sections 44(2) and (3) and 47(1) as applied by those sections (further evidence in relation to claims);

(c) section 49 (adjudication of claim);

(d) section 50 (entitlement to vote and draw dividend);

(e) section 60 (liabilities and rights of co-obligants); and

(f) Schedule 1 except paragraphs 2, 4 and 6 (determination of amount of creditor's claim).

(2) For any reference in the provisions of the Bankruptcy Act, as applied by these Rules, to any expression in column 1 below, there shall be substituted a reference to the expression in column 2 opposite thereto -

Column 1	Column 2
Interim trustee	Liquidator
Permanent trustee	Liquidator
Sequestration	Liquidation
Date of sequestration	Date of commencement of winding up within the meaning of section 129
Debtor	Company
Debtor's assets	Company's assets
Accountant in Bankruptcy	The court
Commissioners	Liquidation committee
Sheriff	The court
Preferred debts	Preferential debts within the meaning of section 386

Claims in foreign currency

4.17.—(1) A creditor may state the amount of his claim in a currency other than sterling where -

(a) his claim is constituted by decree or other order made by a court ordering the company to pay to the creditor a sum expressed in a currency other than sterling, or

(b) where it is not so constituted, his claim arises from a contract or bill of exchange in terms of which payment is or may be required to be made by the company to the creditor in a currency other than sterling.

(2) Where a claim is stated in currency other than sterling for the purpose of the preceding paragraph, it shall be converted into sterling at the rate of exchange for that other currency at the mean of the buying and selling spot rates prevailing in the London market at the close of business on the date of commencement of winding up.

CHAPTER 6

THE LIQUIDATOR

SECTION A: APPOINTMENT AND FUNCTIONS OF LIQUIDATOR

Appointment of liquidator by the court

4.18.—(1) This Rule applies where a liquidator is appointed by the court under section 138(1) (appointment of interim liquidator), 138(5) (no person appointed or nominated by the meetings of creditors and contributories), 139(4) (different persons nominated by creditors and contributories) or 140(1) or (2) (liquidation following administration or voluntary arrangement).

(2) The court shall not make the appointment unless and until there is lodged in court a statement to the effect that the person to be appointed is an insolvency practitioner, duly qualified under the Act to be the liquidator, and that he consents so to act.

(3) Thereafter, the court shall send a copy of the order to the liquidator, whose appointment takes effect from the date of the order.

(4) The liquidator shall -

(a) within 7 days of his appointment, give notice of it to the registrar of companies; and *Form 4.9 (Scot)*

(b) within 28 days of his appointment, give notice of it to the creditors and contributories or, if the court so permits, he shall advertise his appointment in accordance with the directions of the court.

(5) In any notice or advertisement to be given by him under this Rule, the liquidator shall -

(a) state whether he intends to summon meetings of creditors and contributories for the purpose of establishing a liquidation committee or whether he proposes to summon only a meeting of creditors for that purpose; and

(b) if he does not propose to summon any meeting, set out the powers of the creditors under section 142(3) to require him to summon such a meeting.

Appointment by creditors or contributories

4.19.—(1) This Rule applies where a person is nominated for appointment as liquidator under section 139(2) either by a meeting of creditors or by a meeting of contributories.

(2) Subject to section 139(4) the interim liquidator , as chairman of the meeting, or, where the interim liquidator is nominated as liquidator, the chairman of the meeting, shall certify the appointment of a person as liquidator *Form 4.8 (Scot)* by the meeting but not until and unless the person to be appointed has provided him with a written statement to the effect that he is an insolvency practitioner, duly qualified under the Act to be the liquidator and that he consents so to act.

(3) The appointment of the liquidator shall be effective as from the date when his appointment is certified under paragraph (2) by the chairman of the meeting of the creditors or, where no person has been nominated to be liquidator by

that meeting, the chairman of the meeting of the contributories and this date shall be stated in the certificate.

(4) The liquidator shall -

(a) within 7 days of his appointment, give notice of his appointment to the court and to the registrar of companies; and *Form 4.9 (Scot)*

(b) within 28 days of his appointment, give notice of it in a newspaper circulating in the area where the company has its principal place of business, or in such newspaper as he thinks most appropriate for ensuring that it comes to the notice of the company's creditors and contributories.

(5) The provisions of Rule 4.18(5) shall apply to any notice given by the liquidator under this Rule.

(6) Paragraphs (4) and (5) need not be complied with in the case of a liquidator appointed by a company meeting and replaced by another liquidator appointed on the same day by a creditors' meeting.

Authentication of liquidator's appointment

4.20. A copy certified by the clerk of court of any order of court appointing the liquidator or, as the case may be, a copy, certified by the chairman of the meeting which appointed the liquidator, of the certificate of the liquidator's appointment under Rule 4.19(2), shall be sufficient evidence for all purposes and in any proceedings that he has been appointed to exercise the powers and perform the duties of liquidator in the winding up of the company.

Hand-over of assets to liquidator

4.21.—(1) This Rule applies where a person appointed as liquidator ("the succeeding liquidator") succeeds a previous liquidator ("the former liquidator") as the liquidator.

(2) When the succeeding liquidator's appointment takes effect, the former liquidator shall forthwith do all that is required for putting the succeeding liquidator into possession of the assets.

(3) The former liquidator shall give to the succeeding liquidator all such information, relating to the affairs of the company and the course of the winding up, as the succeeding liquidator considers to be reasonably required for the effective discharge by him of his duties as such and shall hand over all books, accounts, statements of affairs, statements of claim and other records and documents in his possession relating to the affairs of the company and its winding up.

Taking possession and realisation of the company's assets

4.22.—(1) Sections 38 and 39(4) and (7) of the Bankruptcy Act shall apply in relation to a liquidation of a company as it applies in relation to a sequestration of a debtor's estate, subject to the modifications specified in paragraph (2) and Rule 4.16(2) and to any other necessary modifications.

(2) For subsection (1) of section 38, there shall be substituted the following section:-

"(1) The liquidator shall -

(a) as soon as may be after his appointment take possession of the whole assets of the company and any property, books, papers or records in the possession or control of the company or to which the company appears to be entitled; and

(b) make up and maintain an inventory and valuation of the assets which he shall retain in the sederunt book.".

SECTION B: REMOVAL AND RESIGNATION; VACATION OF OFFICE

Summoning of meeting for removal of liquidator

4.23.—(1) Subject to section 172(3) and without prejudice to any other method of summoning the meeting, a meeting of creditors for the removal of the liquidator in accordance with section 172(2) shall be summoned by the liquidator if requested to do so by not less than one quarter in value of the creditors.

(2) Where a meeting of creditors is summoned especially for the purpose of removing the liquidator in accordance with section 172(2), the notice summoning it shall draw attention to section 174(4)(*a*) or (*b*) with respect to the liquidator's release.

(3) At the meeting, a person other than the liquidator or his nominee may be elected to act as chairman; but if the liquidator or his nominee is chairman and a resolution has been proposed for the liquidator's removal, the chairman shall not adjourn the meeting without the consent of at least one-half (in value) of the creditors present (in person or by proxy) and entitled to vote.

(4) Where a meeting is to be held or is proposed to be summoned under this Rule, the court may, on the application of any creditor, give directions as to the mode of summoning it, the sending out and return of forms of proxy, the conduct of the meeting, and any other matter which appears to the court to require regulation or control under this Rule.

Procedure on liquidator's removal

4.24.—(1) Where the creditors have resolved that the liquidator be removed, the chairman of the creditors' meeting shall forthwith -

(a) if, at the meeting, another liquidator was not appointed, send a certificate of the liquidator's removal to the court and to the registrar of companies, and
Form 4.10 (Scot)
Form 4.11 (Scot)

(b) otherwise, deliver the certificate to the new liquidator, who shall forthwith send it to the court and to the registrar of companies.
Form 4.10 (Scot)
Form 4.11 (Scot)

(2) The liquidator's removal is effective as from such date as the meeting of the creditors shall determine, and this shall be stated in the certificate of removal.

Release of liquidator on removal

4.25.—(1) Where the liquidator has been removed by a creditors' meeting which has not resolved against his release, the date on which he has his release in terms of section 174(4)(*a*) shall be stated in the certificate of removal before a copy of it is sent to the court and to the registrar of companies under Rule 4.24(1).
Form 4.10 (Scot)
Form 4.11 (Scot)

(2) Where the liquidator is removed by a creditors' meeting which has resolved against his release, or is removed by the court, he must apply to the Accountant *Form 4.12 (Scot)* of Court for his release.

(3) When the Accountant of Court releases the former liquidator, he shall -

(a) issue a certificate of release to the new liquidator who shall send a copy *Form 4.13 (Scot)* of it to the court and to the registrar of companies, and *Form 4.14 (Scot)*

(b) send a copy of the certificate to the former liquidator,

and in this case release of the former liquidator is effective from the date of the certificate.

Removal of liquidator by the court

4.26.—(1) This Rule applies where application is made to the court for the removal of the liquidator, or for an order directing the liquidator to summon a meeting of creditors for the purpose of removing him.

(2) The court may require the applicant to make a deposit or give caution for the expenses to be incurred by the liquidator on the application.

(3) The applicant shall, at least 14 days before the hearing, send to the liquidator a notice stating its date, time and place and accompanied by a copy of the application, and of any evidence which he intends to adduce in support of it.

(4) Subject to any contrary order of the court, the expenses of the application are not payable as an expense of the liquidation.

(5) Where the court removes the liquidator -

(a) it shall send two copies of the order of removal to him;

(b) the order may include such provision as the court thinks fit with respect to matters arising in connection with the removal; and

(c) if the court appoints a new liquidator, Rule 4.18 applies,

and the liquidator, on receipt of the two court orders under sub-paragraph (a), shall send one copy of the order to the registrar of companies, together with *Form 4.11 (Scot)* a notice of his ceasing to act as a liquidator.

Advertisement of removal

4.27. Where a new liquidator is appointed in place of the one removed, Rules 4.19 to 4.21 shall apply to the appointment of the new liquidator except that the notice to be given by the new liquidator under Rule 4.19(4) shall also state - *Form 4.9 (Scot)*

(a) that his predecessor as liquidator has been removed; and

(b) whether his predecessor has been released.

Resignation of liquidator

4.28.—(1) Before resigning his office under section 172(6) the liquidator shall call a meeting of creditors for the purpose of receiving his resignation.

(2) The notice summoning the meeting shall draw attention to section 174(4)(c) and Rule 4.29(4) with respect of the liquidator's release and shall also

49

be accompanied by an account of the liquidator's administration of the winding up, including a summary of his receipts and payments.

(3) Subject to paragraph (4), the liquidator may only proceed under this Rule on the grounds of ill health or because -

(a) he intends ceasing to be in practice as an insolvency practitioner; or

(b) there has been some conflict of interest or change of personal circumstances which precludes or makes impracticable the further discharge by him of the duties of the liquidator.

(4) Where two or more persons are acting as liquidator jointly, any one of them may resign (without prejudice to the continuation in office of the other or others) on the ground that, in his opinion and that of the other or others, it is no longer expedient that there should continue to be the present number of joint liquidators.

Action following acceptance of liquidator's resignation

4.29.—(1) This Rule applies where a meeting is summoned to receive the liquidator's resignation.

(2) If the liquidator's resignation is accepted, it is effective as from such date as the meeting of the creditors may determine and that date shall be stated in the notice given by the liquidator under paragraph (3).

(3) The liquidator, whose resignation is accepted, shall forthwith after the meeting give notice of his resignation to the court as required by section 172(6) and shall send a copy of it to the registrar of companies. *Form 4.15 (Scot) Form 4.6 (Scot)*

(4) The meeting of the creditors may grant the liquidator his release from such date as they may determine. If the meeting resolves against the liquidator having his release, Rule 4.25(2) and (3) shall apply.

(5) Where the creditors have resolved to appoint a new liquidator in place of the one who has resigned, Rules 4.19 to 4.21 shall apply to the appointment of the new liquidator, except that the notice to be given by the new liquidator under Rule 4.19(4) shall also state that his predecessor as liquidator has resigned *Form 4.9 (Scot)* and whether he has been released.

Leave to resign granted by the court

4.30.—(1) If, at a creditors' meeting summoned to receive the liquidator's resignation, it is resolved that it be not accepted, the court may, on the liquidator's application, make an order giving him leave to resign.

(2) The court's order under this Rule may include such provision as it thinks fit with respect to matters arising in connection with the resignation including the notices to be given to the creditors and the registrar of companies and shall *Form 4.16 (Scot)* determine the date from which the liquidator's release is effective.

SECTION C: RELEASE ON COMPLETION OF WINDING UP

Final meeting

4.31.—(1) The liquidator shall give at least 28 days' notice of the final meeting of creditors to be held under section 146. The notice shall be sent to all creditors whose claims in the liquidation have been accepted.

(2) The liquidator's report laid before the meeting shall contain an account of his administration of the winding up, including a summary of his receipts and payments.

(3) At the final meeting, the creditors may question the liquidator with respect to any matter contained in his report, and may resolve against the liquidator having his release.

(4) The liquidator shall within 7 days of the meeting give notice to the court and to the registrar of companies under section 172(8) that the final meeting *Form 4.17 (Scot)* has been held and the notice shall state whether or not he has been released, and be accompanied by a copy of the report laid before the meeting.

(5) If there is no quorum present at the final meeting, the liquidator shall report to the court that a final meeting was summoned in accordance with the Rules, but that there was no quorum present; and the final meeting is then deemed to have been held and the creditors not to have resolved against the liquidator being released.

(6) If the creditors at the final meeting have not resolved against the liquidator having his release, he is released in terms of section 174(4)*(d)*(ii) when he vacates office under section 172(8). If they have so resolved he shall apply for his release to the Accountant of Court, and Rules 4.25(2) and (3) shall apply accordingly.

SECTION D: OUTLAYS AND REMUNERATION

Determination of amount of outlays and remuneration

4.32.—(1) Subject to the provisions of Rules 4.33 to 4.35, claims by the liquidator for the outlays reasonably incurred by him and for his remuneration shall be made in accordance with section 53 of the Bankruptcy Act as applied by Rule 4.68 and as further modified by paragraphs (2) and (3) below.

(2) After section 53(1) of the Bankruptcy Act, there shall be inserted the following subsection:-

"(1A) The liquidator may, at any time before the end of an accounting period, submit to the liquidation committee (if any) an interim claim in respect of that period for the outlays reasonably incurred by him and for his remuneration and the liquidation committee may make an interim determination in relation to the amount of the outlays and remuneration payable to the liquidator and, where they do so, they shall take into account that interim determination when making their determination under subsection (3)*(a)*(ii).".

(3) In section 53(6) of the Bankruptcy Act, for the reference to "subsection (3)*(a)*(ii)" there shall be substituted a reference to "subsection (1A) or (3)*(a)*(ii)".

Recourse of liquidator to meeting of creditors

4.33. If the liquidator's remuneration has been fixed by the liquidation committee and he considers the amount to be insufficient, he may request that it be increased by resolution of the creditors.

Recourse to the court

4.34.—(1) If the liquidator considers that the remuneration fixed for him by the liquidation committee, or by resolution of the creditors, is insufficient, he may apply to the court for an order increasing its amount or rate.

(2) The liquidator shall give at least 14 days' notice of his application to the members of the liquidation committee; and the committee may nominate one or more members to appear or be represented, and to be heard, on the application.

(3) If there is no liquidation committee, the liquidator's notice of his application shall be sent to such one or more of the company's creditors as the court may direct, which creditors may nominate one or more of their number to appear or be represented.

(4) The court may, if it appears to be a proper case, order the expenses of the liquidator's application, including the expenses of any member of the liquidation committee appearing on it, or any creditor so appearing, to be paid as an expense of the liquidation.

Creditors' claim that remuneration is excessive

4.35.—(1) If the liquidator's remuneration has been fixed by the liquidation committee or by the creditors, any creditor or creditors of the company representing in value at least 25 per cent of the creditors may apply to the court for an order that the liquidator's remuneration be reduced, on the grounds that it is, in all the circumstances, excessive.

(2) If the court considers the appliction to be well-founded, it shall make an order fixing the remuneration at a reduced amount or rate.

(3) Unless the court orders otherwise, the expenses of the application shall be paid by the applicant, and are not payable as an expense of the liquidation.

SECTION E: SUPPLEMENTARY PROVISIONS

Liquidator deceased

4.36.—(1) Subject to the following paragraph, where the liquidator has died, it is the duty of his executors or, where the deceased liquidator was a partner *Form 4.18 (Scot)* in a firm, of a partner in that firm to give notice of that fact to the court and to the registrar of companies, specifying the date of death. This does not apply if notice has been given under the following paragraph.

(2) Notice of the death may also be given by any person producing to the *Form 4.18 (Scot)* court and to the registrar of companies a copy of the death certificate.

Loss of qualification as insolvency practitioner

4.37.—(1) This Rule applies where the liquidator vacates office on ceasing to be qualified to act as an insolvency practitioner in relation to the company.

(2) He shall forthwith give notice of his doing so to the court and to the *Form 4.19 (Scot)* registrar of companies.

(3) Rule 4.25(2) and (3) apply as regards the liquidator obtaining his release, as if he had been removed by the court.

Power of court to set aside certain transactions

4.38.—(1) If in the course of the liquidation the liquidator enters into any transaction with a person who is an associate of his, the court may, on the application of any person interested, set the transaction aside and order the liquidator to compensate the company for any loss suffered in consequence of it.

(2) This does not apply if either -

(a) the transaction was entered into with the prior consent of the court, or

(b) it is shown to the court's satisfaction that the transaction was for value, and that it was entered into by the liquidator without knowing, or having any reason to suppose, that the person concerned was an associate.

(3) Nothing in this Rule is to be taken as prejudicing the operation of any rule of law with respect to a trustee's dealings with trust property, or the fiduciary obligations of any person.

Rule against solicitation

4.39.—(1) Where the court is satisfied that any improper solicitation has been used by or on behalf of the liquidator in obtaining proxies or procuring his appointment, it may order that no remuneration be allowed as an expense of the liquidation to any person by whom, or on whose behalf, the solicitation was exercised.

(2) An order of the court under this Rule overrides any resolution of the liquidation committee or the creditors, or any other provision of the Rules relating to the liquidator's remuneration.

CHAPTER 7

THE LIQUIDATION COMMITTEE

Preliminary

4.40. For the purposes of this Chapter -

(a) an "insolvent winding up" takes place where a company is being wound up on grounds which include its inability to pay its debts, and

(b) a "solvent winding up" takes place where a company is being wound up on grounds which do not include that one.

Membership of committee

4.41.—(1) Subject to Rule 4.43 below, the liquidation committee shall consist as follows:-

(a) in the case of any winding up, of at least 3 and not more than 5 creditors of the company, elected by the meeting of creditors held under section 138 or 142 of the Act, and also

(b) in the case of a solvent winding up where the contributories' meeting held under either of those sections so decides, up to 3 contributories, elected by that meeting.

(2) Any creditor of the company (other than one whose debt is fully secured and who has not agreed to surrender his security to the liquidator) is eligible to be a member of the committee, so long as -

(a) he has lodged a claim of his debt in the liquidation, and

(b) his claim has neither been wholly rejected for voting purposes, nor wholly rejected for the purposes of his entitlement so far as funds are available to a dividend.

(3) No person can be a member as both a creditor and a contributory.

(4) A body corporate or a partnership may be a member of the committee, but it cannot act as such otherwise than by a member's representative appointed under Rule 4.48 below.

(5) In this Chapter, members of the committee elected or appointed by a creditors' meeting are called "creditor members", and those elected or appointed by a contributories' meeting are called "contributory members".

(6) Where the Deposit Protection Board exercises the right (under section 28 of the Banking Act 1979(**a**)) to be a member of the committee, the Board is to be regarded as an additional creditor member.

Formalities of establishment

4.42.—(1) The liquidation committee shall not come into being, and accordingly cannot act, until the liquidator has issued a certificate of its due constitution.

*Form 4.20
(Scot)*

(2) If the chairman of the meeting which resolves to establish the committee is not the liquidator, he shall forthwith give notice of the resolution to the

---

(**a**) 1979 c.37.

liquidator (or, as the case may be, the person appointed as liquidator by the same meeting), and inform him of the names and addresses of the persons elected to be members of the committee.

(3) No person may act as a member of the committee unless and until he has agreed to do so; and the liquidator's certificate of the committee's due constitution shall not be issued until at least the minimum number of persons in accordance with Rule 4.41 who are to be members of it have agreed to act, but shall be issued forthwith thereafter. *Form 4.20 (Scot)*

(4) As and when the others (if any) agree to act, the liquidator shall issue an amended certificate. *Form 4.20 (Scot)*

(5) The certificate (and any amended certificate) shall be sent by the liquidator to the registrar of companies. *Form 4.22 (Scot)*

(6) If after the first establishment of the committee there is any change in its membership, the liquidator shall report the change to the registrar of companies. *Form 4.22 (Scot)*

Committee established by contributories

4.43.—(1) The following applies where the creditors' meeting under section 138 or 142 of the Act does not decide that a liquidation committee should be established or decides that a liquidation committee should not be established.

(2) A meeting of contributories under section 138 or 142 may appoint one of their number to make application to the court for an order to the liquidator that a further creditors' meeting be summoned for the purpose of establishing a liquidation committee; and -

    (a) the court may, if it thinks that there are special circumstances to justify it, make that order, and

    (b) the creditors' meeting summoned by the liquidator in compliance with the order is deemed to have been summoned under section 142.

(3) If the creditors' meeting so summoned does not establish a liquidation committee, a meeting of contributories may do so.

(4) The committee shall then consist of at least 3, and not more than 5, contributories elected by that meeting; and Rule 4.42 shall apply to such a committee with the substitution of references to contributories for references to creditors.

Obligations of liquidator to committee

4.44.—(1) Subject as follows, it is the duty of the liquidator to report to the members of the liquidation committee all such matters as appear to him to be, or as they have indicated to him as being, of concern to them with respect to the winding up.

(2) In the case of matters so indicated to him by the committee, the liquidator need not comply with any request for information where it appears to him that -

    (a) the request is frivolous or unreasonable, or

    (b) the cost of complying would be excessive, having regard to the relative importance of the information, or

(c) there are not sufficient assets to enable him to comply.

(3) Where the committee has come into being more than 28 days after the appointment of the liquidator, he shall report to them, in summary form, what actions he has taken since his appointment, and shall answer all such questions as they may put to him regarding his conduct of the winding up hitherto.

(4) A person who becomes a member of the committee at any time after its first establishment is not entitled to require a report to him by the liquidator, otherwise than in summary form, of any matters previously arising.

(5) Nothing in this Rule disentitles the committee, or any member of it, from having access to the liquidator's cash book and sederunt book, or from seeking an explanation of any matter within the committee's responsibility.

Meetings of the committee

4.45.—(1) Subject as follows, meetings of the liquidation committee shall be held when and where determined by the liquidator.

(2) The liquidator shall call a first meeting of the committee to take place within 3 months of his appointment or of the committee's establishment (whichever is the later); and thereafter he shall call a meeting -

(a) if so requested by a creditor member of the committee or his representative (the meeting then to be held within 21 days of the request being received by the liquidator), and

(b) for a specified date, if the committee has previously resolved that a meeting be held on that date.

(3) The liquidator shall give 7 days' written notice of the time and place of any meeting to every member of the committee (or his representative, if designated for that purpose), unless in any case the requirement of the notice has been waived by or on behalf of any member. Waiver may be signified either at or before the meeting.

The chairman at meetings

4.46.—(1) The chairman at any meeting of the liquidation committee shall be the liquidator, or a person nominated by him to act.

(2) A person so nominated must be either -

(a) a person who is qualified to act as an insolvency practitioner in relation to the company, or

(b) an employee of the liquidator or his firm who is experienced in insolvency matters.

Quorum

4.47. A meeting of the committee is duly constituted if due notice of it has been given to all the members, and at least 2 creditor members or, in the case of a committee of contributories, 2 contributory members are present or represented.

Committee members' representatives

4.48.—(1) A member of the liquidation committee may, in relation to the business of the committee, be represented by another person duly authorised by him for that purpose.

(2) A person acting as a committee-member's representative must hold a mandate entitling him so to act (either generally or specially) and signed by or on behalf of the committee-member.

(3) The chairman at any meeting of the committee may call on a person claiming to act as a committee-member's representative to produce his mandate and may exclude him if it appears that his mandate is deficient.

(4) No member may be represented by a body corporate or by a partnership, or by an undischarged bankrupt.

(5) No person shall -

(a) on the same committee, act at one and the same time as representative of more than one committee-member, or

(b) act both as a member of the committee and as representative of another member.

(6) Where a member's representative signs any document on the member's behalf, the fact that he so signs must be stated below his signature.

Resignation

4.49. A member of the liquidation committee may resign by notice in writing delivered to the liquidator.

Termination of membership

4.50. Membership of the liquidation committee of any person is automatically terminated if -

(a) his estate is sequestrated or he becomes bankrupt or grants a trust deed for the benefit of or makes a composition with his creditors, or

(b) at 3 consecutive meetings of the committee he is neither present nor represented (unless at the third of those meetings it is resolved that this Rule is not to apply in his case),or

(c) that creditor being a creditor member, he ceases to be, or is found never to have been a creditor.

Removal

4.51. A creditor member of the committee may be removed by resolution at a meeting of creditors; and a contributory member may be removed by a resolution of a meeting of contributories.

Vacancy (creditor members)

4.52.—(1) The following applies if there is a vacancy among the creditor members of the committee.

(2) The vacancy need not be filled if the liquidator and a majority of the remaining creditor members so agree, provided that the total number of members does not fall below the minimum required by Rule 4.41(1).

(3) The liquidator may appoint any creditor, who is qualified under the Rules to be a member of the committee, to fill the vacancy, if a majority of the other creditor members agrees to the appointment, and the creditor concerned consents to act.

(4) Alternatively, a meeting of creditors may resolve that a creditor be appointed (with his consent) to fill the vacancy. In this case, at least 14 days' notice must have been given of the resolution to make such an appointment (whether or not of a person named in the notice).

(5) Where the vacancy is filled by an appointment made by a creditors' meeting at which the liquidator is not present, the chairman of the meeting shall report to the liquidator the appointment which has been made.

Vacancy (contributory members)

4.53.—(1) The following applies if there is a vacancy among the contributory members of the committee.

(2) The vacancy need not be filled if the liquidator and a majority of the remaining contributory members so agree, provided that , in the case of a committee of contributory members only, the total number of members does not fall below the minimum required by Rule 4.41(1) or, as the case may be, 4.59(4).

(3) The liquidator may appoint any contributory member (being qualified under the Rules to be a member of the committee) to fill the vacancy, if a majority of the other contributory members agree to the appointment, and the contributory concerned consents to act.

(4) Alternatively, a meeting of contributories may resolve that a contributory be appointed (with his consent) to fill the vacancy. In this case, at least 14 days' notice must have been given of the resolution to make such an appointment (whether or not of a person named in the notice).

(5) Where the vacancy is filled by an appointment made by a contributories' meeting at which the liquidator is not present, the chairman of the meeting shall report to the liquidator the appointment which has been made.

Voting rights and resolutions

4.54.—(1) At any meeting of the committee, each member of it (whether present himself, or by his representative) has one vote; and a resolution is passed when a majority of the creditor members present or represented have voted in favour of it.

(2) Subject to the next paragraph, the votes of contributory members do not count towards the number required for passing a resolution, but the way in which they vote on any resolution shall be recorded.

(3) Paragraph (2) does not apply where, by virtue of Rule 4.43(4) or 4.59, the only members of the committee are contributories. In that case the committee is to be treated for voting purposes as if all its members were creditors.

(4) Every resolution passed shall be recorded in writing, either separately or as part of the minutes of the meeting. The record shall be signed by the chairman and kept as part of the sederunt book.

Resolutions by post

4.55.—(1) In accordance with this Rule, the liquidator may seek to obtain the agreement of members of the liquidation committee to a resolution by sending to every member (or his representative designated for the purpose) a copy of the proposed resolution.

(2) Where the liquidator makes use of the procedure allowed by this Rule, he shall send out to members of the committee or their representatives (as the case may be) a statement incorporating the resolution to which their agreement is sought, each resolution (if more than one) being set out in a separate document.

(3) Any creditor member of the committee may, within 7 business days from the date of the liquidator sending out a resolution, require him to summon a meeting of the committee to consider the matters raised by the resolution.

(4) In the absence of such a request, the resolution is deemed to have been passed by the committee if and when the liquidator is notified in writing by a majority of the creditor members that they concur with it.

(5) A copy of every resolution passed under this Rule, and a note that the committee's concurrence was obtained, shall be kept in the sederunt book.

Liquidator's reports

4.56.—(1) The liquidator shall, as and when directed by the liquidation committee (but not more often than once in any period of 2 months), send a written report to every member of the committee setting out the position generally as regards the progress of the winding up and matters arising in connection with it, to which the liquidator considers the committee's attention should be drawn.

(2) In the absence of such directions by the committee, the liquidator shall send such a report not less often than once in every period of 6 months.

(3) The obligations of the liquidator under this Rule are without prejudice to those imposed by Rule 4.44.

Expenses of members, etc.

4.57.—(1) The liquidator shall defray any reasonable travelling expenses directly incurred by members of the liquidation committee or their representatives in respect of their attendance at the committee's meetings, or otherwise on the committee's business, as an expense of the liquidation.

(2) Paragraph (1) does not apply to any meeting of the committee held within 3 months of a previous meeting.

Dealings by committee-members and others

4.58.—(1) This Rule applies to -

(a) any member of the liquidation committee;

(b) any committee-member's representative;

(c) any person who is an associate of a member of the committee or of a committee-member's representative; and

(d) any person who has been a member of the committee at any time in the last 12 months.

(2) Subject as follows, a person to whom this Rule applies shall not enter into any transaction whereby he -

(a) receives out of the company's assets any payment for services given or goods supplied in connection with the liquidation, or

(b) obtains any profit from the liquidation, or

(c) acquires any part of the company's assets.

(3) Such a transaction may be entered into by a person to whom this Rule applies -

(a) with the prior leave of the court, or

(b) if he does so as a matter of urgency, or by way of performance of a contract in force before the date on which the company went into liquidation, and obtains the court's leave for the transaction, having applied for it without undue delay, or

(c) with the prior sanction of the liquidation committee, where it is satisfied (after full disclosure of the circumstances) that the transaction will be on normal commercial terms.

(4) Where in the committee a resolution is proposed that sanction be accorded for a transaction to be entered into which, without that sanction or the leave of the court, would be in contravention of this Rule, no member of the committee, and no representative of a member, shall vote if he is to participate directly or indirectly in the transaction.

(5) The court may, on the application of any person interested, -

(a) set aside a transaction on the ground that it has been entered into in contravention of this Rule, and

(b) make with respect to it such other order as it thinks fit, including (subject to the following paragraph) an order requiring a person to whom this Rule applies to account for any profit obtained from the transaction and compensate the company's assets for any resultant loss.

(6) In the case of a person to whom this Rule applies as an associate of a member of the committee or of a committee-member's representative, the court shall not make any order under paragraph (5), if satisfied that he entered into the relevant transaction without having any reason to suppose that in doing so he would contravene this Rule.

(7) The expenses of an application to the court for leave under this Rule are not payable as an expense of the liquidation, unless the court so orders.

Composition of committee when creditors paid in full

4.59.—(1) This Rule applies if the liquidator issues a certificate that the creditors have been paid in full, with interest in accordance with section 189. *Form 4.23 (Scot)*

60

(2) The liquidator shall forthwith send a copy of the certificate to the registrar of companies.

Form 4.24
(Scot)

(3) The creditor members of the liquidation committee shall cease to be members of the committee.

(4) The committee continues in being unless and until abolished by decision of a meeting of contributories, and (subject to the next paragraph) so long as it consists of at least 2 contributory members.

(5) The committee does not cease to exist on account of the number of contributory members falling below 2, unless and until 28 days have elapsed since the issue of the liquidator's certificate under paragraph (1), but at any time when the committee consists of less than 2 contributory members, it is suspended and cannot act.

(6) Contributories may be co-opted by the liquidator, or appointed by a contributories' meeting, to be members of the committee; but the maximum number of members is 5.

(7) The foregoing Rules in this Chapter continue to apply to the liquidation committee (with any necessary modifications) as if all the members of the committee were creditor members.

CHAPTER 8

THE LIQUIDATION COMMITTEE WHERE WINDING UP FOLLOWS IMMEDIATELY ON ADMINISTRATION

Preliminary

4.60.—(1) The Rules in this Chapter apply where -

(a) the winding up order has been made immediately upon the discharge of an administration order under Part II of the Act, and

(b) the court makes an order under section 140(1) appointing as liquidator the person who was previously the administrator.

(2) In this Chapter the expressions "insolvent winding up", "solvent winding up", "creditor member", and "contributory member" each have the same meaning as in Chapter 7.

Continuation of creditors' committee

4.61.—(1) If under section 26 a creditors' committee has been established for the purposes of the administration, then (subject as follows in this Chapter) that committee continues in being as the liquidation committee for the purposes of the winding up, and -

(a) it is deemed to be a committee established as such under section 142, and

(b) no action shall be taken under subsections (1) to (4) of that section to establish any other.

(2) This Rule does not apply if, at the time when the court's order under section 140(1) is made, the committee under section 26 consists of less than 3 members; and a creditor who was, immediately before the date of that order, a member of such a committee ceases to be a member on the making of the order if his debt is fully secured (and he has not agreed to surrender his security to the liquidator).

Membership of committee

4.62.—(1) Subject as follows, the liquidation committee shall consist of at least 3, and not more than 5, creditors of the company, elected by the creditors' meeting held under section 26 or (in order to make up numbers or fill vacancies) by a creditors' meeting summoned by the liquidator after the company goes into liquidation.

(2) In the case of a solvent winding up, the liquidator shall, on not less than 21 days' notice, summon a meeting of contributories, in order to elect (if it so wishes) contributory members of the liquidation committee, up to 3 in number.

Liquidator's certificate

4.63.—(1) The liquidator shall issue a certificate of the liquidation committee's continuance specifying the persons who are, or are to be, members of it.

Form 4.21 (Scot)

(2) It shall be stated in the certificate whether or not the liquidator has summoned a meeting of contributories under Rule 4.62(2), and whether (if so) the meeting has elected contributories to be members of the committee.

(3) Pending the issue of the liquidator's certificate, the committee is suspended and cannot act.

(4) No person may act, or continue to act, as a member of the committee unless and until he has agreed to do so; and the liquidator's certificate shall not be issued until at least the minimum number of persons required under Rule 4.62 to form a committee elected, whether under Rule 4.62 above or under section 26, have signified their agreement.

(5) As and when the others signify their agreement, the liquidator shall issue an amended certificate. *Form 4.21 (Scot)*

(6) The liquidator's certificate (or, as the case may be, the amended certificate) shall be sent by him to the registrar of companies. *Form 4.22 (Scot)*

(7) If subsequently there is any change in the committee's membership, the liquidator shall report the change to the registrar of companies. *Form 4.22 (Scot)*

Obligations of liquidator to committee

4.64.—(1) As soon as may be after the issue of the liquidator's certificate under Rule 4.63, the liquidator shall report to the liquidation committee what actions he has taken since the date on which the company went into liquidation.

(2) A person who becomes a member of the committee after that date is not entitled to require a report to him by the liquidator, otherwise than in a summary form, of any matters previously arising.

(3) Nothing in this Rule disentitles the committee, or any member of it, from having access to the sederunt book (whether relating to the period when he was administrator, or to any subsequent period), or from seeking an explanation of any matter within the committee's responsibility.

Application of Chapter 7

4.65. Except as provided elsewhere in this Chapter, Rules 4.44 to 4.59 of Chapter 7 shall apply to a liquidation committee established under this Chapter from the date of issue of the certificate under Rule 4.63 as if it had been established under section 142. *Form 4.21 (Scot)*

63

CHAPTER 9

DISTRIBUTION OF COMPANY'S ASSETS BY LIQUIDATOR

Order of priority in distribution

4.66.—(1) The funds of the company's assets shall be distributed by the liquidator to meet the following expenses and debts in the order in which they are mentioned:-

(a) the expenses of the liquidation;

(b) any preferential debts within the meaning of section 386 (excluding any interest which has been accrued thereon to the date of commencement of the winding up within the meaning of section 129);

(c) ordinary debts, that is to say a debt which is neither a secured debt nor a debt mentioned in any other sub-paragraph of this paragraph;

(d) interest at the official rate on -

(i) the preferential debts, and

(ii) the ordinary debts,

between the said date of commencement of the winding up and the date of payment of the debt; and

(e) any postponed debt.

(2) In the above paragraph -

(a) "postponed debt" means a creditor's right to any alienation which has been reduced or restored to the company's assets under section 242 or to the proceeds of sale of such an alienation; and

(b) "official rate" shall be construed in accordance with subsection (4) of section 189 and, for the purposes of paragraph (a) of that subsection, as applied to Scotland by subsection (5), the rate specified in the Rules shall be 15 per centum per annum.

(3) The expenses of the liquidation mentioned in sub-paragraph (a) of paragraph (1) are payable in the order of priority mentioned in Rule 4.67.

(4) Subject to the provisions of section 175, any debt falling within any of sub-paragraphs (b) to (e) of paragraph (1) shall have the same priority as any other debt falling within the same sub-paragraph and, where the funds of the company's assets are inadequate to enable the debts mentioned in this sub-paragraph to be paid in full, they shall abate in equal proportions.

(5) Any surplus remaining, after all expenses and debts mentioned in paragraph (1) have been paid in full, shall (unless the articles of the company otherwise provide) be distributed among the members according to their rights and interests in the company.

(6) Nothing in this Rule shall affect -

(a) the right of a secured creditor which is preferable to the rights of the liquidator; or

(b) any preference of the holder of a lien over a title deed or other document which has been delivered to the permanent trustee in accordance with a requirement under section 38(4) of the Bankruptcy Act , as applied by Rule 4.22.

Order of priority of expenses of liquidation

4.67.—(1) Subject to section 156 and paragraph (2), the expenses of the liquidation are payable out of the assets in the following order of priority -

(a) any outlays properly chargeable or incurred by the provisional liquidator or liquidator in carrying out his functions in the liquidation, except those outlays specifically mentioned in the following sub-paragraphs;

(b) the cost, or proportionate cost, of any caution provided by a provisional liquidator, liquidator or special manager in accordance with the Act or the Rules;

(c) the remuneration of the provisional liquidator (if any);

(d) the expenses of the petitioner in the liquidation, and of any person appearing in the petition whose expenses are allowed by the court;

(e) the remuneration of the special manager (if any);

(f) any allowance made by the liquidator under Rule 4.9(1) (expenses of statement of affairs);

(g) the remuneration or emoluments of any person who has been employed by the liquidator to perform any services for the company, as required or authorised by or under the Act or the Rules;

(h) the remuneration of the liquidator determined in accordance with Rule 4.32;

(i) the amount of any capital gains tax on chargeable gains accruing on the realisation of any asset of the company (without regard to whether the realisation is effected by the liquidator, a secured creditor or otherwise).

(2) In any winding up by the court which follows immediately on a voluntary winding up (whether members' voluntary or creditors' voluntary), such outlays and remuneration of the voluntary liquidator as the court may allow, shall have the same priority as the outlays mentioned in sub-paragraph *(a)* of paragraph (1).

(3) Nothing in this Rule applies to or affects the power of any court, in proceedings by or against the company, to order expenses to be paid by the company, or the liquidator; nor does it affect the rights of any person to whom such expenses are ordered to be paid.

Application of the Bankruptcy Act

4.68.—(1) Sections 52, 53 and 58 of the Bankruptcy Act shall apply in relation to the liquidation of a company as they apply in relation to a sequestration of a debtor's estate, subject to the modifications specified in Rules 4.16(2) and 4.32(2) and (3) and the following paragraph and to any other necessary modifications.

(2) In section 52, the following modifications shall be made:-

(a) in subsection (4)*(a)* for the reference to "the debts mentioned in subsection (1)*(a)* to *(d)*", there shall be substituted a reference to the expenses of the winding up mentioned in Rule 4.67(1)*(a)*;

(b) in subsection (5), the words "with the consent of the commissioners or if there are no commissioners of the Accountant in Bankruptcy" should be deleted; and .

(c) in subsection (7) and (8) for the references to section 48(5) and 49(6)*(b)* there should be substituted a reference to those sections as applied by Rule 4.16(1).

CHAPTER 10

SPECIAL MANAGER

Appointment and remuneration

4.69.—(1) This Chapter applies to an application under section 177 by the liquidator or, where one has been appointed, by the provisional liquidator for the appointment of a person to be special manager (references in this Chapter to the liquidator shall be read as including the provisional liquidator).

(2) An application shall be supported by a report setting out the reasons for the appointment. The report shall include the applicant's estimate of the value of the assets in respect of which the special manager is to be appointed.

(3) The order of the court appointing the special manager shall specify the duration of his appointment, which may be for a period of time or until the occurrence of a specified event. Alternatively the order may specify that the duration of the appointment is to be subject to a further order of the court.

(4) The appointment of a special manager may be renewed by order of the court.

(5) The special manager's remuneration shall be fixed from time to time by the court.

(6) The acts of the special manager are valid notwithstanding any defect in his appointment or qualifications.

Caution

4.70.—(1) The appointment of the special manager does not take effect until the person appointed has found (or, being allowed by the court to do so, has undertaken to find) caution to the person who applies for him to be appointed.

(2) It is not necessary that caution be found for each separate company liquidation; but it may be found either specially for a particular liquidation, or generally for any liquidation in relation to which the special manager may be employed as such.

(3) The amount of the caution shall be not less than the value of the assets in respect of which he is appointed, as estimated by the applicant in his report under Rule 4.69.

(4) When the special manager has found caution to the person applying for his appointment, that person shall certify the adequacy of the security and notify the court accordingly.

(5) The cost of finding caution shall be paid in the first instance by the special manager; but -

(a) where a winding up order is not made, he is entitled to be reimbursed out of the property of the company, and the court may make an order on the company accordingly, and

(b) where a winding up order has been or is subsequently made, he is entitled to be reimbursed as an expense of the liquidation.

Failure to find or to maintain caution

4.71.—(1) If the special manager fails to find the required caution within the time stated for that purpose by the order appointing him, or any extension of that time that may be allowed, the liquidator shall report the failure to the court, which may thereupon discharge the order appointing the special manager.

(2) If the special manager fails to maintain his caution the liquidator shall report his failure to the court, which may thereupon remove the special manager and make such order as it thinks fit as to expenses.

(3) If an order is made under this Rule removing the special manager, or recalling the order appointing him, the court shall give directions as to whether any, and if so what, steps should be taken to appoint another special manager in his place.

Accounting

4.72.—(1) The special manager shall produce accounts containing details of his receipts and payments for the approval of the liquidator.

(2) The accounts shall be in respect of 3-month periods for the duration of the special manager's appointment (or for a lesser period if his appointment terminates less than 3 months from its date, or from the date to which the last accounts were made up).

(3) When the accounts have been approved, the special manager's receipts and payments shall be added to those of the liquidator.

Termination of appointment

4.73.—(1) The special manager's appointment terminates if the winding up petition is dismissed or, if a provisional liquidator having been appointed, he is discharged without a winding up order having been made.

(2) If the liquidator is of opinion that the employment of the special manager is no longer necessary or profitable for the company, he shall apply to the court for directions, and the court may order the special manager's appointment to be terminated.

(3) The liquidator shall make the same application if a resolution of the creditors is passed, requesting that the appointment be terminated.

CHAPTER 11

PUBLIC EXAMINATION OF COMPANY OFFICERS AND OTHERS

Notice of order for public examination

4.74. Where the court orders the public examination of any person under section 133(1), then, unless the court otherwise directs, the liquidator shall give at least 14 days' notice of the time and place of the examination to the persons specified in paragraphs *(c)* to *(e)* of section 133(4) and the liquidator may, if he thinks fit, cause notice of the order to be given, by public advertisement in one or more newspapers circulating in the area of the principal place of business of the company, at least 14 days before the date fixed for the examination but there shall be no such advertisement before at least 7 days have elapsed from the date when the person to be examined was served with the order.

Order on request by creditors or contributories

4.75.—(1) A request to the liquidator by a creditor or creditors or contributory or contributories under section 133(2) shall be made in writing and be accompanied by -

   (a) a list of the creditors (if any) concurring with the request and the amounts of their respective claims in the liquidation, or (as the case may be) of the contributories (if any) so concurring, with their respective values, and

   (b) from each creditor or contributory concurring, written confirmation of his concurrence.

(2) The request must specify the name of the proposed examinee, the relationship which he has, or has had, to the company and the reasons why his examination is requested.

(3) Before an application to the court is made on the request, the requisitionists shall deposit with the liquidator such sum as the latter may determine to be appropriate by way of caution for the expenses of the hearing of a public examination, if ordered.

(4) Subject as follows, the liquidator shall, within 28 days of receiving the request, make the application to the court required by section 133(2).

(5) If the liquidator is of opinion that the request is an unreasonable one in the circumstances, he may apply to the court for an order relieving him from the obligation to make the application otherwise required by that subsection.

(6) If the court so orders, and the application for the order was made *ex parte*, notice of the order shall be given forthwith by the liquidator to the requisitionists. If the application for an order is dismissed, the liquidator's application under section 133(2) shall be made forthwith on conclusion of the hearing of the application first mentioned.

(7) Where a public examination of the examinee has been ordered by the court on a creditors' or contributories' requisition under this Rule the court may order that the expenses of the examination are to be paid, as to a specified proportion, out of the caution under paragraph (3), instead of out of the assets.

CHAPTER 12

MISCELLANEOUS

Limitation

4.76. The provisions of section 8(5) and 22(8), as read with section 73(5), of the Bankruptcy (Scotland) Act 1985 (presentation of petition or submission of claim to bar effect of limitation of actions) shall apply in relation to the liquidation as they apply in relation to a sequestration, subject to the modifications specified in Rule 4.16(2) and to any other necessary modifications.

Dissolution after winding up

4.77. Where the court makes an order under section 204(5) or 205(5), the person on whose application the order was made shall deliver to the registrar of companies a copy of the order. *Form 4.28 (Scot)*

CHAPTER 13

COMPANY WITH PROHIBITED NAME

Preliminary

4.78. The Rules in this Chapter -

(a) relate to the leave required under section 216 (restriction on re-use of name of company in insolvent liquidation) for a person to act as mentioned in section 216(3) in relation to a company with a prohibited name, and

(b) prescribe the cases excepted from that provision, that is to say, those in which a person to whom the section applies may so act without that leave.

Application for leave under section 216(3)

4.79. When considering an application for leave under section 216, the court may call on the liquidator, or any former liquidator, of the liquidating company for a report of the circumstances in which that company became insolvent, and the extent (if any) of the applicant's apparent responsibility for its doing so.

First excepted case

4.80.—(1) Where a company ("the successor company") acquires the whole, or substantially the whole, of the business of an insolvent company, under arrangements made by an insolvency practitioner acting as its liquidator, administrator or receiver, or as supervisor of a voluntary arrangement under Part I of the Act, the successor company may for the purposes of section 216 give notice under this Rule to the insolvent company's creditors.

(2) To be effective, the notice must be given within 28 days from the completion of the arrangements to all creditors of the insolvent company of whose addresses the successor is aware in that period; and it must specify -

(a) the name and registered number of the insolvent company and the circumstances in which its business has been acquired by the successor company,

(b) the name which the successor company has assumed, or proposes to assume for the purpose of carrying on the business, if that name is or will be a prohibited name under section 216, and

(c) any change of name which it has made, or proposes to make, for that purpose under section 28 of the Companies Act.

(3) The notice may name a person to whom section 216 may apply as having been a director or shadow director of the insolvent company, and give particulars as to the nature and duration of that directorship, with a view to his being a director of the successor company or being otherwise associated with its management.

(4) If the successor company has effectively given notice under this Rule to the insolvent company's creditors, a person who is so named in the notice may act in relation to the successor company in any of the ways mentioned in section 216(3), notwithstanding that he has not the leave of the court under that section.

Second excepted case

4.81.—(1) In the circumstances specified below, a person to whom section 216 applies as having been a director or shadow director of the liquidating company may act in any of the ways mentioned in section 216(3), notwithstanding that he has not the leave of the court under that section.

(2) Those circumstances are that -

(a) he applies to the court for leave, not later than 7 days from the date on which the company went into liquidation, and

(b) leave is granted by the court not later than 6 weeks from that date.

Third excepted case

4.82. The court's leave under section 216(3) is not required where the company there referred to, though known by a prohibited name within the meaning of the section, -

(a) has been known by that name for the whole of the period of 12 months ending with the day before the liquidating company went into liquidation, and

(b) has not at any time in those 12 months been dormant within the meaning of section 252(5) of the Companies Act.

PART 5

CREDITORS' VOLUNTARY WINDING UP

Application of Part 4

5. The provisions of Part 4 shall apply in a creditors' voluntary winding up of a company as they apply in a winding up by the court subject to the modifications specified in Schedule 1 and to any other necessary modifications.

PART 6

MEMBERS' VOLUNTARY WINDING UP

Application of Part 4

6. The provisions of Part 4, which are specified in Schedule 2, shall apply in relation to a members' voluntary winding up of a company as they apply in a winding up by the court, subject to the modifications specified in Schedule 2 and to any other necessary modifications.

PART 7

PROVISIONS OF GENERAL APPLICATION

CHAPTER 1

MEETINGS

Scope of Chapter 1

7.1.—(1) This Chapter applies to any meetings held in insolvency proceedings other than meetings of a creditors' committee in administration or receivership, or of a liquidation committee.

(2) The Rules in this Chapter shall apply to any such meeting subject to any contrary provision in the Act or in the Rules, or to any direction of the court.

Summoning of meetings

7.2.—(1) In fixing the date, time and place for a meeting, the person summoning the meeting ("the convenor") shall have regard to the convenience of the persons who are to attend.

(2) Meetings shall in all cases be summoned for commencement between 10.00 and 16.00 hours on a business day, unless the court otherwise directs.

Notice of meeting

7.3.—(1) The convenor shall give not less than 21 days' notice of the date, time and place of the meeting to every person known to him as being entitled to attend the meeting.

(2) In paragraph (1), for the reference to 21 days, there shall be substituted a reference to 14 days in the following cases:-

(a) any meeting of the company or of its creditors summoned under section 3 (to consider directors' proposal for voluntary arrangement);

(b) a meeting of the creditors under section 23(1)*(b)* or 25(2)*(b)* (to consider administrator's proposals or proposed revisions); and

(c) a meeting of creditors under section 67(2) (meeting of unsecured creditors in receivership).

(3) The convenor may also publish notice of the date, time and place of the meeting in a newspaper circulating in the area of the principal place of business of the company or in such other newspaper as he thinks most appropriate for ensuring that it comes to the notice of the persons who are entitled to attend the meeting. In the case of a creditors' meeting summoned by the administrator under section 23(1)*(b)*, the administrator shall publish such a notice.

(4) Any notice under this Rule shall state -

(a) the purpose of the meeting;

(b) the persons who are entitled to attend and vote at the meeting;

(c) the effects of Rule 7.9 or, as the case may be, 7.10 (Entitlement to Vote) and of the relevant provisions of Rule 7.12 (Resolutions);

(d) in the case of a meeting of creditors or contributories, that proxies may be lodged at or before the meeting and the place where they may be lodged; and

(e) in the case of a meeting of creditors, that claims may be lodged by those who have not already done so at or before the meeting and the place where they may be lodged.

Where a meeting of creditors is summoned specially for the purpose of removing the liquidator in accordance with section 171(2) or 172(2), or of receiving his resignation under Rule 4.28, the notice summoning it shall also include the information required by Rule 4.23(2) or, as the case may be, 4.28(2).

(5) With the notice given under paragraph (1), the convenor shall also send out a proxy form.

(6) In the case of any meeting of creditors or contributories, the court may order that notice of the meeting be given by public advertisement in such form as may be specified in the order and not by individual notice to the persons concerned. In considering whether to make such an order, the court shall have regard to the cost of the public advertisement, to the amount of the assets available and to the extent of the interest of creditors or contributories or any particular class of either.

Additional notices in certain cases

7.4.—(1) This Rule applies where a company goes, or proposes to go, into liquidation and it is -

(a) a recognised bank or licensed institution within the meaning of the Banking Act 1979(**a**), or

(b) an institution to which sections 16 and 18 of that Act apply as if it were a licensed institution.

(2) Notice of any meeting of the company at which it is intended to propose a resolution for its voluntary winding up shall be given by the directors to the Bank of England ("the Bank") and to the Deposit Protection Board ("the Board") as such notice is given to members of the company.

(3) Where a creditors' meeting is summoned by the liquidator under section 95 or 98, the same notice of meeting must be given to the Bank and Board as is given to the creditors under this Chapter.

(4) Where the company is being wound up by the court, notice of the first meetings of creditors and contributories within the meaning of Rule 4.12 shall be given to the Bank and the Board by the liquidator.

(5) Where in any winding up a meeting of creditors or contributories is summoned for the purpose of -

(a) receiving the liquidator's resignation, or

(b) removing the liquidator, or

(c) appointing a new liquidator,

(**a**) 1979 c.37.

the person summoning the meeting and giving notice of it shall also give notice to the Bank and the Board.

(6) The Board is entitled to be represented at any meeting of which it is required by this Rule to be given notice; and Schedule 3 has effect with respect to the voting rights of the Board at such a meeting.

Chairman of meetings

7.5.—(1) The chairman at any meeting of creditors in insolvency proceedings shall be the responsible insolvency practitioner, or a person nominated by him in writing.

(2) A person nominated under this Rule must be either -

(a) a person who is qualified to act as an insolvency practitioner in relation to the company, or

(b) an employee of the administrator, receiver or liquidator, as the case may be, or his firm who is experienced in insolvency matters.

(3) This Rule also applies to meetings of contributories in a liquidation.

(4) At the first meeting of creditors or contributories in a winding up by the court, the interim liquidator shall be the chairman except that, where a resolution is proposed to appoint the interim liquidator to be the liquidator, another person may be elected to act as chairman for the purpose of choosing the liquidator.

(5) This Rule is subject to Rule 4.23(3) (meeting for removal of liquidator).

Meetings requisitioned

7.6.—(1) Subject to paragraph (8), this Rule applies to any request by a creditor or creditors for a meeting of creditors -

(a) to an administrator under section 17(3), or

(b) to a liquidator under section 142(3), 171(3) or 172(3),

or under any other provision of the Act or the Rules.

(2) Any such request shall be accompanied by -

(a) a list of any creditors concurring with the request, showing the amounts of the respective claims against the company of the creditor making the request and the concurring creditors;

(b) from each creditor concurring, written confirmation of his concurrence; and

(c) a statement of the purpose of the proposed meeting.

(3) If the administrator or, as the case may be, the liquidator considers the request to be properly made in accordance with the Act or the Rules, he shall summon a meeting of the creditors to be held on a date not more than 35 days from the date of his receipt of the request.

(4) Expenses of summoning and holding a meeting under this Rule shall be paid by the creditor or creditors making the request, who shall deposit with the administrator caution for their payment.

(5) The sum to be deposited shall be such as the administrator or, as the case may be, the liquidator may determine and he shall not act without the deposit having been made.

(6) The meeting may resolve that the expenses of summoning and holding it are to be payable out of the assets of the company as an expense of the administration or, as the case may be, the liquidation.

(7) To the extent that any caution deposited under this Rule is not required for the payment of expenses of summoning and holding the meeting, it shall be repaid to the person or persons who made it.

(8) This Rule applies to requests by a contributory or contributories for a meeting of contributories, with the modification that, for the reference in paragraph (2) to the creditors' respective claims, there shall be substituted a reference to the contributories' respective values (being the amounts for which they may vote at any meeting).

(9) This Rule is without prejudice to the powers of the court under Rule 4.67(2) (voluntary winding up succeeded by winding up by the court).

Quorum

7.7.—(1) Subject to the next paragraph, a quorum is -

(a) in the case of a creditors' meeting, at least one creditor entitled to vote;

(b) in the case of a meeting of contributories, at least 2 contributories so entitled, or all the contributories, if their number does not exceed 2.

(2) For the purposes of this Rule, the reference to the creditor or contributories necessary to constitute a quorum is not confined to those persons present or duly represented under section 375 of the Companies Act but includes those represented by proxy by any person (including the chairman).

Adjournment

7.8.—(1) This Rule applies to meetings of creditors and to meetings of contributories.

(2) If, within a period of 30 minutes from the time appointed for the commencement of a meeting, a quorum is not present, then, unless the chairman otherwise decides, the meeting shall be adjourned to the same time and place in the following week or, if that is not a business day, to the business day immediately following.

(3) In the course of any meeting, the chairman may, in his discretion, and shall, if the meeting so resolves, adjourn it to such date, time and place as seems to him to be appropriate in the circumstances.

(4) Paragraph (3) is subject to Rule 4.23(3) where the liquidator or his nominee is chairman and a resolution has been proposed for the liquidator's removal.

(5) An adjournment under paragraph (1) or (2) shall not be for a period of more than 21 days.

(6) Where a meeting is adjourned, any proxies given for the original meeting may be used at the adjourned meeting.

Entitlement to vote (creditors)

7.9.—(1) This Rule applies to a creditors' meeting in any insolvency proceedings.

(2) A creditor is entitled to vote at any meeting if he has submitted his claim to the responsible insolvency practitioner and his claim has been accepted in whole or in part.

(3) Chapter 5 of Part 4 (claims in liquidation) shall apply for the purpose of determining a creditor's entitlement to vote at any creditors' meeting in any insolvency proceedings as it applies for the purpose of determining a creditor's entitlement to vote at a meeting of creditors in a liquidation, subject to the modifications specified in the following paragraphs and to any other necessary modification.

(4) For any reference in the said Chapter 5, or in any provision of the Bankruptcy Act as applied by Rule 4.16(1), to -

(a) the liquidator, there shall be substituted a reference to the supervisor, administrator or receiver, as the case may be;

(b) the liquidation, there shall be substituted a reference to the voluntary arrangement, administration or receivership as the case may be;

(c) the date of commencement of winding up, there shall be substituted a reference -

(i) in the case of a meeting in a voluntary arrangement, to the date of the meeting or, where the company is being wound up or is subject to an administration order, the date of its going into liquidation or, as the case may be, of the administration order; and

(ii) in the case of a meeting in the administration or receivership, to the date of the administration order or, as the case may be, the date of appointment of the receiver;

(5) In the application to meetings of creditors other than in liquidation proceedings of Schedule 1 to the Bankruptcy Act, paragraph 5(2) and (3) (secured creditors) shall not apply.

(6) This Rule is subject to Rule 7.4(6) and Schedule 3.

Entitlement to vote (members and contributories)

7.10.—(1) Members of a company or contributories at their meetings shall vote according to their rights attaching to their shares respectively in accordance with the articles of association.

(2) In the case of a meeting of members of the company in a voluntary arrangement, where no voting rights attach to a member's share, he is nevertheless entitled to vote either for or against the proposal or any modification of it.

(3) Reference in this Rule to a person's share include any other interests which he may have as a member of the company.

Chairman of meeting as proxy holder

7.11.—(1) Where the chairman at a meeting of creditors or contributories holds a proxy which requires him to vote for a particular resolution and no other person proposes that resolution -

(a) he shall propose it himself, unless he considers that there is good reason for not doing so, and

(b) if he does not propose it, he shall forthwith after the meeting notify the person who granted him the proxy of the reason why he did not do so.

(2) At any meeting in a voluntary arrangement, the chairman shall not, by virtue of any proxy held by him, vote to increase or reduce the amount of the remuneration or expenses of the nominee or the supervisor of the proposed arrangement, unless the proxy specifically directs him to vote in that way.

Resolutions

7.12.—(1) Subject to any contrary provision in the Act or the Rules, at any meeting of creditors, contributories or members of a company, a resolution is passed when a majority in value of those voting, in person or by proxy, have voted in favour of it.

(2) In a voluntary arrangement, at a creditors' meeting for any resolution to pass approving any proposal or modification, there must be at least three quarters in value of the creditors present or represented and voting, in person or by proxy, in favour of the resolution.

(3) In a liquidation, in the case of a resolution for the appointment of a liquidator -

(a) if, on any vote, there are two nominees for appointment, the person for whom a majority in value has voted shall be appointed;

(b) if there are three or more nominees, and one of them has a clear majority over both or all the others together, that one is appointed; and

(c) in any other case, the chairman of the meeting shall continue to take votes (disregarding at each vote any nominee who has withdrawn and, if no nominee has withdrawn, the nominee who obtained the least support last time), until a clear majority is obtained for any one nominee.

The chairman may, at any time, put to the meeting a resolution for the joint appointment of any two or more nominees.

(4) Where a resolution is proposed which affects a person in respect of his remuneration or conduct as a responsible insolvency practitioner, the vote of that person, or of his firm or of any partner or employee of his shall not be reckoned in the majority required for passing the resolution. This paragraph applies with respect to a vote given by a person either as creditor or contributory or member or as proxy for a creditor, contributory, or member.

Report of meeting

7.13.—(1) The chairman at any meeting shall cause a report to be made of the proceedings at the meeting which shall be signed by him.

(2) The report of the meeting shall include -

(a) a list of all the creditors or, as the case may be, contributories who attended the meeting, either in person or by proxy;

(b) a copy of every resolution passed; and

(c) if the meeting established a creditors' committee or a liquidation committee, as the case may be, a list of the names and addresses of those elected to be members of the committee.

(3) The chairman shall keep a copy of the report of the meeting as part of the sederunt book in the insolvency proceedings.

CHAPTER 2

PROXIES AND COMPANY REPRESENTATION

Definition of "proxy"

7.14.—(1) For the purposes of the Rules, a person ("the principal") may authorise another person ("the proxy-holder") to attend, speak and vote as his representative at meetings of creditors or contributories or of the company in insolvency proceedings, and any such authority is referred to as a proxy.

(2) A proxy may be given either generally for all meetings in insolvency proceedings or specifically for any meeting or class of meetings.

(3) Only one proxy may be given by the principal for any one meeting; and it may only be given to one person, being an individual aged 18 or over. The principal may nevertheless nominate one or more other such persons to be proxy-holder in the alternative in the order in which they are named in the proxy.

(4) Without prejudice to the generality of paragraph (3), a proxy for a particular meeting may be given to whoever is to be the chairman of the meeting.

(5) A proxy may require the holder to vote on behalf of the principal on matters arising for determination at any meeting, or to abstain, either as directed or in accordance with the holder's own discretion; and it may authorise or require the holder to propose, in the principal's name, a resolution to be voted on by the meeting.

Form of proxy

7.15.—(1) With every notice summoning a meeting of creditors or contributories or of the company in insolvency proceedings there shall be sent out forms of proxy.

(2) A form of proxy shall not be sent out with the name or description of any person inserted in it.

(3) A proxy shall be in the form sent out with the notice summoning the meeting or in a form substantially to the same effect.

(4) A form of proxy shall be filled out and signed by the principal, or by some person acting under his authority and, where it is signed by someone other than the principal, the nature of his authority shall be stated on the form.

Use of proxy at meeting

7.16.—(1) A proxy given for a particular meeting may be used at any adjournment of that meeting.

(2) A proxy may be lodged at or before the meeting at which it is to be used.

(3) Where the responsible insolvency practitioner holds proxies to be used by him as chairman of the meeting, and some other person acts as chairman, the other person may use the insolvency practitioner's proxies as if he were himself proxy-holder.

Retention of proxies

7.17.—(1) Proxies used for voting at any meeting shall be retained by the chairman of the meeting.

(2) The chairman shall deliver the proxies forthwith after the meeting to the responsible insolvency practitioner (where he was not the chairman).

(3) The responsible insolvency practitioner shall retain all proxies in the sederunt book.

Right of inspection

7.18.—(1) The responsible insolvency practitioner shall, so long as proxies lodged with him are in his hands, allow them to be inspected at all reasonable times on any business day, by -

(a) the creditors, in the case of proxies used at a meeting of creditors,

(b) a company's members or contributories, in the case of proxies used at a meeting of the company or of its contributories.

(2) The reference in paragraph (1) to creditors is -

(a) in the case of a company in liquidation, those creditors whose claims have been accepted in whole or in part, and

(b) in any other case, persons who have submitted in writing a claim to be creditors of the company concerned,

but in neither case does it include a person whose claim has been wholly rejected for purposes of voting, dividend or otherwise.

(3) The right of inspection given by this Rule is also exercisable, in the case of an insolvent company, by its directors.

(4) Any person attending a meeting in insolvency proceedings is entitled, immediately before or in the course of the meeting, to inspect proxies and associated documents to be used in connection with that meeting.

Proxy-holder with financial interest

7.19.—(1) A proxy-holder shall not vote in favour of any resolution which would directly or indirectly place him, or any associate of his, in a position to receive any remuneration out of the insolvent estate, unless the proxy specifically directs him to vote in that way.

(2) This Rule applies also to any person acting as chairman of a meeting and using proxies in that capacity; and in its application to him, the proxy-holder is deemed an associate of his.

Representation of corporations

7.20.—(1) Where a person is authorised under section 375 of the Companies Act to represent a corporation at a meeting of creditors or contributories, he shall produce to the chairman of the meeting a copy of the resolution from which he derives his authority.

(2) The copy resolution must be executed in accordance with the provisions of section 36(3) of the Companies Act, or certified by the secretary or a director of the corporation to be a true copy.

CHAPTER 3

MISCELLANEOUS

Giving of notices, etc.

7.21.—(1) All notices required or authorised by or under the Act or the Rules to be given, sent or delivered must be in writing, unless it is otherwise provided, or the court allows the notice to be sent or given in some other way.

(2) Any reference in the Rules to giving, sending or delivering a notice or any such document means, without prejudice to any other way and unless it is otherwise provided, that the notice or document may be sent by post, and that, subject to Rule 7.22, any form of post may be used. Personal service of the notice or document is permissible in all cases.

(3) Where under the Act or the Rules a notice or other document is required or authorised to be given, sent or delivered by a person ("the sender") to another ("the recipient"), it may be given, sent or delivered by any person duly authorised by the sender to do so to any person duly authorised by the recipient to receive or accept it.

(4) Where two or more persons are acting jointly as the responsible insolvency practitioner in any proceedings, the giving, sending or delivering of a notice or document to one of them is to be treated as the giving, sending or delivering of a notice or document to each or all.

Sending by post

7.22.—(1) For a document to be properly sent by post, it must be contained in an envelope addressed to the person to whom it is to be sent, and pre-paid for either first or second class post.

(2) Where first class post is used, the document is to be deemed to be received on the second business day after the date of posting, unless the contrary is shown.

(3) Where second class post is used, the document is to be deemed to be received on the fourth business day after the date of posting, unless the contrary is shown.

Certificate of giving notice, etc.

7.23.—(1) Where in any proceedings a notice or document is required to be given, sent or delivered by the responsible insolvency practitioner, the date of giving, sending or delivery of it may be proved by means of a certificate signed by him or on his behalf by his solicitor, or a partner or an employee of either of them, that the notice or document was duly given, posted or otherwise sent, or delivered on the date stated in the certificate.

(2) In the case of a notice or document to be given, sent or delivered by a person other than the responsibile insolvency practitioner, the date of giving, sending or delivery of it may be proved by means of a certificate by that person that he gave, posted or otherwise sent or delivered the notice or document on the date stated in the certificate, or that he instructed another person (naming him) to do so.

(3) A certificate under this Rule may be endorsed on a copy of the notice to which it relates.

(4) A certificate purporting to be signed by or on behalf of the responsible insolvency practitioner, or by the person mentioned in paragraph (2), shall be deemed, unless the contrary is shown, to be sufficient evidence of the matters stated therein.

Validity of proceedings

7.24. Where in accordance with the Act or the Rules a meeting of creditors or other persons is summoned by notice, the meeting is presumed to have been duly summoned and held, notwithstanding that not all those to whom the notice is to be given have received it.

Evidence of proceedings at meetings

7.25. A report of proceedings at a meeting of the company or of the company's creditors or contributories in any insolvency proceedings, which is signed by a person describing himself as the chairman of that meeting, shall be deemed, unless the contrary is shown, to be sufficient evidence of the matters contained in that report.

Right to list of creditors and copy documents

7.26.—(1) Paragraph (2) applies to -

(a) proceedings under Part II of the Act (company administration), and

(b) proceedings in a creditors' voluntary winding up, or a winding up by the court.

(2) Subject to Rule 7.27, in any such proceedings, a creditor who has the right to inspect documents also has the right to require the responsible insolvency practitioner to furnish him with a list of the company's creditors and the amounts of their respective debts.

(3) Subject to Rule 7.27, where a person has the right to inspect documents, the right includes that of taking copies of those documents, on payment of the appropriate fee.

(4) In this Rule, the appropriate fee means 15 pence per A4 or A5 page and 30 pence per A3 page.

Confidentiality of documents

7.27.—(1) Where, in any insolvency proceedings, the responsible insolvency practitioner considers, in the case of a document forming part of the records of those proceedings, -

(a) that it should be treated as confidential, or

(b) that it is of such a nature that its disclosure would be calculated to be injurious to the interests of the company's creditors or, in the case of the winding up of a company, its members or the contributories in its winding up,

he may decline to allow it to be inspected by a person who would otherwise be entitled to inspect it.

(2) The persons who may be refused the right to inspect documents under this Rule by the responsible insolvency practitioner include the members of a creditors' committee in administration or in receivership, or of a liquidation committee.

(3) Where under this Rule the responsible insolvency practitioner refuses inspection of a document, the person who made that request may apply to the court for an order to overrule the refusal and the court may either overrule it altogether, or sustain it, either unconditionally or subject to such conditions, if any, as it thinks fit to impose.

Insolvency practitioner's caution

7.28.—(1) Wherever under the Rules any person has to appoint, or certify the appointment of, an insolvency practitioner to any office, he is under a duty to satisfy himself that the person appointed or to be appointed has caution for the proper performance of his functions.

(2) It is the duty -

(a) of the creditors' committee in administration or in receivership,

(b) of the liquidation committee in companies winding up, and

(c) of any committee of creditors established for the purposes of a voluntary arrangement under Part I of the Act,

to review from time to time the adequacy of the responsible insolvency practitioner's caution.

(3) In any insolvency proceedings the cost of the responsible insolvency practitioner's caution shall be paid as an expense of the proceedings.

Punishment of offences

7.29.—(1) Schedule 4 has effect with respect to the way in which contraventions of the Rules are punishable on conviction.

(2) In that Schedule -

(a) the first column specifies the provision of the Rules which creates an offence;

(b) in relation to each such offence, the second column describes the general nature of the offence;

(c) the third column indicates its mode of trial, that is to say whether the offence is punishable on conviction on indictment, or on summary conviction, or either in the one way or the other;

(d) the fourth column shows the maximum punishment by way of fine or imprisonment which may be imposed on a person convicted of the offence in the mode of trial specified in relation to it in the third column (that is to say, on indictment or summarily), a reference to a period of years or months being to a maximum term of imprisonment of that duration; and

(e) the fifth column shows (in relation to an offence for which there is an entry in that column) that a person convicted of the offence after continued contravention is liable to a daily default fine; that is to say, he is liable on a second or subsequent conviction of the offence to the fine specified

85

in that column for each day on which the contravention is continued (instead of the penalty specified for the offence in the fourth column of that Schedule).

(3) Section 431 (summary proceedings), as it applies to Scotland, has effect in relation to offences under the Rules as to offences under the Act.

Forms for use in insolvency proceedings

7.30. The forms contained in Schedule 5, with such variations as circumstances require, are the forms to be used for the purposes of the provisions of the Act or the Rules which are referred to in those forms.

Fees, expenses, etc.

7.31. All fees, costs, charges and other expenses incurred in the course of insolvency proceedings are to be regarded as expenses of those proceedings.

Power of court to cure defects in procedure

7.32.—(1) Section 63 of the Bankruptcy Act (power of court to cure defects in procedure) shall apply in relation to any insolvency proceedings as it applies in relation to sequestration, subject to the modifications specified in paragraph (2) and to any other necessary modifications.

(2) For any reference in the said section 63 to any expression in column 1 below, there shall be substituted a reference to the expression in column 2 opposite thereto:-

Column 1	Column 2
This Act or any regulations made under it	The Act or the Rules
Permanent trustee	Responsible insolvency practitioner
Sequestration process	Insolvency proceedings
Debtor	Company
Sheriff	The court
Person who would be eligible to be elected under section 24 of this Act	Person who would be eligible to act as a responsible insolvency practitioner

Sederunt book

7.33.—(1) The responsible insolvency practitioner shall maintain a sederunt book during his term of office for the purpose of providing an accurate record of the administration of each insolvency proceedings.

(2) Without prejudice to the generality of the above paragraph, there shall be inserted in the sederunt book a copy of anything required to be recorded in it by any provision of the Act or of the Rules.

(3) The responsible insolvency practitioner shall make the sederunt book available for inspection at all reasonable hours by any interested person.

(4) Any entry in the sederunt book shall be sufficient evidence of the facts stated therein, except where it is founded on by the responsible insolvency practitioner in his own interest.

Michael Howard,
Parliamentary Under Secretary of State.

Department of Trade and Industry,
1 Victoria Street,
London.
10th November 1986.

MODIFICATIONS OF PART 4 IN RELATION TO CREDITORS' VOLUNTARY WINDING UP

1. The following paragraphs describe the modifications to be made to the provisions of Part 4 in their application by Rule 5 to a creditors' voluntary winding up of a company.

General

2. Any reference, in any provision in Part 4, which is applied to a creditors' voluntary winding up, to any other Rule is a reference to that Rule as so applied.

Chapter 1 (Provisional liquidator)

3. This Chapter shall not apply.

Chapter 2 (Statement of affairs)

Rules 4.7 and 4.8

4. For these Rules, there shall be substituted the following:-

"**4.7.**—(1) This Rule applies with respect to the statement of affairs made out by the liquidator under section 95(3) (or as the case may be) by the directors under section 99(1).

(2) The statement of affairs shall be in the form required by Rule 7.30 and Schedule 5.   *Form 4.4 (Scot)*

(3) Where the statement of affairs is made out by the directors under section 99(1), it shall be sent by them to the liquidator, when appointed.

(4) The liquidator shall insert a copy of the statement of affairs made out under this Rule in the sederunt book.".

Rule 4.9

5. For this Rule, there shall be substituted -

"Expenses of statement of affairs

4.9.—(1) Payment may be made as an expense of the liquidation, either before or after the commencement of the winding up, of any reasonable and necessary expenses of preparing the statement of affairs under section 99.

(2) Where such a payment is made before the commencement of the winding up, the director presiding at the creditors' meeting held under section 98 shall inform the meeting of the amount of the payment and the identity of the person to whom it was made.

(3) The liquidator appointed under section 100 may make such a payment (subject to the next paragraph); but if there is a liquidation committee, he must give the committee at least 7 days' notice of his intention to make it.

(4) Such a payment shall not be made by the liquidator to himself, or to any associate of his, otherwise than with the approval of the liquidation committee, the creditors, or the court.

(5) This Rule is without prejudice to the powers of the court under Rule 4.67(2) (voluntary winding up succeeded by winding up by the court).".

Chapter 3 (Information)

Rule 4.10

6. For this Rule, there shall be substituted the following:-

"Information to creditors and contributories

4.10. The liquidator shall, within 28 days of a meeting held under section 95 or 98, send to creditors and contributories of the company -

(a) a copy or summary of the statement of affairs, and

(b) a report of the proceedings at the meeting.".

Chapter 4 (Meetings of creditors and contributories)

Rule 4.12

7. This Rule shall not apply.

Rule 4.14

8. After this Rule, there shall be inserted the following:-

"Expenses of meeting under section 98

4.14A.—(1) Payment may be made out of the company's assets as an expense of the liquidation, either before or after the commencement of the winding up, of any reasonable and necessary expenses incurred in connection with the summoning, advertisement and holding of a creditors' meeting under section 98.

(2) Where any such payments are made before the commencement of the winding up, the director presiding at the creditors' meeting shall inform the meeting of their amount and the identity of the persons to whom they were made.

(3) The liquidator appointed under section 100 may make such a payment (subject to the next paragraph); but if there is a liquidation committee, he must give the committee at least 7 days' notice of his intention to make the payment.

(4) Such a payment shall not be made by the liquidator to himself, or to any associate of his, otherwise than with the approval of the liquidation committee, the creditors, or the court.

(5) This Rule is without prejudice to the powers of the court under Rule 4.67(2) (voluntary winding up succeeded by winding up by the court).".

Rule 4.15

9. In paragraph (5), for the reference to section 129, there shall be substituted a reference to section 86.

Rule 4.16

10. In paragraph (2), for the reference to section 129, there shall be substituted a reference to section 86.

Chapter 6 (The liquidator)

Rule 4.18

11.—(1) For paragraph (1), there shall be substituted the following:-

"(1) This Rule applies where the liquidator is appointed by the court under section 100(3) or 108.".

(2) Paragraphs 4*(a)* and 5 shall be deleted.

Rule 4.19

12.—(1) For paragraphs (1) to (3) there shall be substituted the following:-

"(1) This Rule applies where a person is nominated for appointment as liquidator under section 100(1) either by a meeting of the creditors or by a meeting of the company.

(2) Subject as follows, the chairman of the meeting shall certify the appointment, *Form 4.8 (Scot)* but not unless and until the person to be appointed has provided him with a written statement to the effect that he is an insolvency practitioner, duly qualified under the Act to be the liquidator and that he consents so to act. The liquidator's appointment is effective from the date of the certificate.

(3) The chairman shall forthwith send the certificate to the liquidator, who shall *Form 4.8 (Scot)* keep it in the sederunt book.".

(2) Paragraphs(4)*(a)* and (5) shall not apply.

(3) In paragraph (6), for the reference to paragraphs (4) and (5), there shall be substituted a reference to paragraphs (3) and (4).

Rule 4.23

13.—(1) In paragraph (1), for the references to section 172(2) and (3), there shall be substituted a reference to section 171(2) and (3).

(2) In paragraph (2), for the references to section 172(2) and 174(4)*(a)* or *(b)*, there shall be substituted a reference to section 171(2) and 173(2)*(a)* or *(b)*.

Rule 4.24

14. In this Rule the references to the court shall be deleted.

Rule 4.25

15. In paragraph (1), for the reference to section 174(4)*(a)*, there shall be substituted a reference to section 173(2)*(a)*, and the reference to the court shall be deleted.

Rule 4.28

16.—(1) In paragraph (1), for the reference to section 172(6), there shall be substituted a reference to section 171(5).

(2) In paragraph (2), for the reference to section 174(4)*(c)*, there shall be substituted a reference to section 173(2)*(c)*.

Rule 4.29

17. In this Rule for paragraph (3) there shall be substituted the following:-

"(3) The liquidator, whose resignation is accepted, shall forthwith after the meeting give notice of his resignation to the registrar of companies as required by section *Form 4.16 (Scot)* 171(5).".

Rule 4.31

18. For this Rule, substitute the following:-

"*Final Meeting*

4.31.—(1) The liquidator shall give at least 28 days' notice of the final meeting of creditors to be held under section 106. The notice shall be sent to all creditors whose claims in the liquidation have been accepted.

(2) At the final meeting, the creditors may question the liquidator with respect to any matter contained in the account required under that section and may resolve against the liquidator having his release.

(3) The liquidator shall, within 7 days of the meeting, give notice to the registrar of companies under section 171(6) that the final meeting has been held. The notice shall state whether or not he has been released. Form 4.17 (Scot)

(4) If the creditors at the final meeting have not resolved against the liquidator having his release, he is released in terms of section 173(2)*(e)*(ii) when he vacates office under section 171(6). If they have so resolved, he must obtain his release from the Accountant of Court and Rule 4.25(2) and (3) shall apply accordingly.".

Rule 4.36

19. For the reference to the court there shall be substituted a reference to the liquidation committee (if any) or a member of that committee.

Rule 4.37

20.—(1) In paragraph (2), the reference to the court shall be omitted.

(2) At the end of this Rule, there shall be inserted the following:-

"Vacation of office on making of winding up order

4.37A. Where the liquidator vacates office in consequence of the court making a winding up order against the company, Rule 4.25(2) and (3) apply as regards the liquidator obtaining his release, as if he had been removed by the court.".

Chapter 7 (The liquidation committee)

Rule 4.40

21. This Rule shall not apply.

Rule 4.41

22. For paragraph (1) there shall be substituted the following:-

"(1) The committee must have at least 3 members before it can be established.".

Rule 4.43

23. This Rule shall not apply.

Rule 4.47

24. For this Rule, there shall be substituted the following:-

"Quorum

4.47. A meeting of the committee is duly constituted if due notice of it has been given to all the members and at least 2 members are present or represented.".

Rule 4.53

25. After paragraph (4) there shall be inserted the following:-

"(4A) Where the contributories make an appointment under paragraph (4), the creditor members of the committee may, if they think fit, resolve that the person appointed ought not to be a member of the committee; and -

(a) that person is not then, unless the court otherwise directs, qualified to act as a member of the committee, and

(b) on any application to the court for a direction under this paragraph the court may, if it thinks fit, appoint another person (being a contributory) to fill the vacancy on the committee.".

Rule 4.54

26. Paragraphs (2) and (3) shall not apply.

91

Rule 4.55

27. In paragraphs (3) and (4), the word "creditor" shall be omitted.

Chapter 8 (The liquidation committee where winding up follows immediately on administration)

28. This Chapter shall not apply.

Chapter 9 (Distribution of company's assets by liquidator)

Rule 4.66

29.—(1) At the beginning of paragraph (1), insert the following:-

"Subject to the provision of section 107,".

(2) In paragraph (1)*(b)*, for the reference to section 129, there shall be substituted a reference to section 86.

Chapter 10 (Special manager)

Rule 4.70

30. For paragraph (5), there shall be substituted the following:-

"(5) The cost of finding caution shall be paid in the first instance by the special manager; but he is entitled to be reimbursed out of the assets as an expense of the liquidation.".

Rule 4.71

31. Paragraph (1) shall not apply.

Chapter 11 (Public examination of company officers and others)

32. This Chapter shall not apply.

Chapter 12 (Miscellaneous)

Rule 4.77

33. This Rule shall not apply.

APPLICATION OF PART 4 IN RELATION TO MEMBERS' VOLUNTARY WINDING UP

1. The following paragraphs describe the provisions of Part 4 which, subject to the modifications set out in those paragraphs and any other necessary modifications, apply to a members' voluntary winding up.

General

2. Any reference in any provision of Part 4, which is applied to a members' voluntary winding up, to any other Rule is a reference to that Rule as so applied.

Chapter 3 (Information)

Rule 4.11

3. This Rule shall apply.

Chapter 6 (The liquidator)

Rule 4.18

4.—(1) This Rule shall apply subject to the following modifications.

(2) For paragraph (1), there shall be substituted the following:-

"(1) This Rule applies where the liquidator is appointed by the court under section 108.".

(3) Paragraphs 4 and 5 shall be deleted.

Rule 4.19

5.—(1) This Rule shall apply subject to the following modifications.

(2) For paragraphs (1) to (3) there shall be substituted the following:-

"(1) This Rule applies where the liquidator is appointed by a meeting of the company.

(2) Subject as follows, the chairman of the meeting shall certify the appointment, but not unless and until the person to be appointed has provided him with a written statement to the effect that he is an insolvency practitioner, duly qualified under the Act to be the liquidator and that he consents so to act. The liquidator's appointment is effective from the date of the certificate. *Form 4.8 (Scot)*

(3) The chairman shall forthwith send the certificate to the liquidator, who shall keep it in the sederunt book.". *Form 4.8 (Scot)*

(3) Paragraphs 4(*a*), (5) and (6) shall be deleted.

Rules 4.20 to 4.22

6. These Rules shall apply.

Rule 4.26

7. This Rule shall apply except that in paragraph (1) for the reference to "creditors" there shall be substituted the words "the company".

Rule 4.27

8. This Rule shall apply.

93

Rule 4.28

9.—(1) This Rule shall apply subject to the following modifications.

(2) In paragraph (1) -

(a) for the reference to section 172(6), there shall be substituted a reference to section 171(5), and

(b) for the reference to a meeting of creditors, there shall be substituted a reference to a meeting of the company.

(3) In paragraph (2) -

(a) for reference to section 174(4)(*c*) there shall be substituted a reference to section 173(2)(*c*), and

(b) for the reference to Rule 4.29(4), there shall be substituted a reference to Rule 4.28A.

(4) After paragraph (4) there shall be inserted the following paragraphs:-

"(5) The notice of the liquidator's resignation required by section 171(5) shall be given by him to the registrar of companies forthwith after the meeting. *Form 4.18 (Scot)*

(6) Where a new liquidator is appointed in place of the one who has resigned, the former shall, in giving notice of his appointment, state that his predecessor has resigned and whether he has been released.".

(5) After this Rule, there shall be inserted the following Rule:-

"*Release of resigning or removed liquidator*

4.28A.—(1) Where the liquidator resigns, he has his release from the date on which he gives notice of his resignation to the registrar of companies. *Form 4.16 (Scot)*

(2) Where the liquidator is removed by a meeting of the company, he shall forthwith give notice to the registrar of companies of his ceasing to act. *Form 4.11 (Scot)*

(3) Where the liquidator is removed by the court, he must apply to the Accountant of Court for his release. *Form 4.12 (Scot)*

(4) Where the Accountant of Court gives the release, he shall certify it accordingly, and send the certificate to the registrar of companies. *Form 4.13 (Scot) Form 4.14 (Scot)*

(5) A copy of the certificate shall be sent by the Accountant of Court to the former liquidator, whose release is effective from the date of the certificate.". *Form 4.13 (Scot)*

Rule 4.36

10. This Rule shall apply, except that for any reference to the court, there shall be substituted a reference to the directors of the company or any one of them.

Rule 4.37

11.—(1) This Rule shall apply subject to the following modifications.

(2) In paragraph (2), the reference to the court shall be omitted.

(3) For paragraph (3), there shall be substituted the following:-

"(3) Rule 4.28A applies as regards the liquidator obtaining his release, as if he had been removed by the court.".

(4) At the end of this Rule, there shall be inserted the following:-

"*Vacation of office on making of winding up order*

4.37A. Where the liquidator vacates office in consequence of the court making a winding up order against the company, Rule 4.28A applies as regards the liquidator obtaining his release, as if he had been removed by the court.".

Rule 4.38

12. This Rule shall apply.

Rule 4.39

13. This Rule shall apply.

Chapter 10 (Special manager)

14.—(1) This Chapter shall apply subject to the following modifications..

(2) In Rule 4.70 for paragraph (5), there shall be substituted the following:-

"(5) The cost of finding caution shall be paid in the first instance by the special manager; but he is entitled to be reimbursed out of the assets as an expense of the liquidation.".

(3) In Rule 4.71, paragraph (1) shall not apply.

DEPOSIT PROTECTION BOARD'S VOTING RIGHTS

1. This Schedule applies where Rule 7.4 does.

2. In relation to any meeting at which the Deposit Protection Board is under Rule 7.4 entitled to be represented, the Board may submit in the liquidation, instead of a claim, a written statement of voting rights ("the statement").

3. The statement shall contain details of:-

(a) the names of creditors of the company in respect of whom an obligation of the Board has arisen or may reasonably be expected to arise as a result of the liquidation or proposed liquidation;

(b) the amount of the obligation so arising; and

(c) the total amount of all such obligations specified in the statement.

4. The Board's statement shall, for the purpose of voting at a meeting (but for no other purpose), be treated in all respects as if it were a claim.

5. Any voting rights which a creditor might otherwise exercise at a meeting in respect of a claim against the company are reduced by a sum equal to the amount of that claim in relation to which the Board, by virtue of its having submitted a statement, is entitled to exercise voting rights at that meeting.

6. The Board may from time to time submit a further statement, and, if it does so, that statement supersedes any statement previously submitted.

PUNISHMENT OF OFFENCES UNDER THE RULES

Note: In the fourth and fifth columns of this Schedule, "the statutory maximum" means the prescribed sum under section 289B(6) of the Criminal Procedure (Scotland) Act 1975 (c.21).

Rule creating offence	General nature of offence	Mode of prosecution	Punishment	Daily default fine (where applicable)
In Part 1, Rule 1.24	False representation or fraud for purpose of obtaining members' or creditors' consent to proposal for voluntary arrangement	1. On indictment 2. Summary	7 years or a fine, or both 6 months or the statutory maximum, or both	
In Part 2, Rule 2.17(4)	Administrator failing to send notification as to progress of administration	Summary	One-fifth of the statutory maximum	One-fiftieth of the statutory maximum
In Part 3, Rule 3.9(5)	Receiver failing to send notification as to progress of receivership	Summary	One-fifth of the statutory maximum	One-fiftieth of the statutory maximum

G

FORMS

The Insolvency Act 1986   **Form 1.1 (Scot)**

Notice of Report of a Meeting Approving Voluntary Arrangement

S4(6)

Pursuant to section 4(6) of the Insolvency Act 1986 and Rule 1.17(5) of the Insolvency (Scotland) Rules 1986

To the Registrar of Companies

For official use

Company number

Name of Company

(a) Insert name of company

(a)

(b) Insert full name and address

I (b)

(c) Insert date

the chairman of a meeting held in pursuance of section 4 of the Insolvency Act 1986 on (c) _____ enclose a copy of my report of the said meeting.

Signed _____ Date _____

Presentor's name, address and reference (if any)

For Official use

Liquidation Section	Post Room

Rule 1.20

The Insolvency Act 1986

Form 1.2 (Scot)

Notice of Order of Revocation or Suspension of Voluntary Arrangement

Pursuant to section 6 of the Insolvency Act 1986 and Rule 1.20(5) of the Insolvency (Scotland) Rules 1986

R1.20

To the Registrar of Companies

For official use

Company number

Name of Company

(a) Insert name of company

(a)

(b) Insert full names and address(es)

I/We (b)

(c) Insert date

(d) Delete as applicable

enclose a copy of the order of the court dated (c) _____

(d) revoking/suspending the voluntary arrangement approved on (c) _____

Signed _____ Date _____

Presentor's name, address and reference (if any)

For Official use

Liquidation Section

Post Room

100

Rule 1.21

The Insolvency Act 1986

Form 1.3 (Scot)

R1.21(2)(b)

Notice of Voluntary Arrangement Supervisor's Abstract of Receipts and Payments

Pursuant to Rule 1.21(2)(b) of the Insolvency (Scotland) Rules 1986

To the Registrar of Companies

For official use

Company number

Name of Company

(a) Insert name of company

(a)

(b) Insert full name(s) and address(es)

I/We (b)

supervisor(s) of a voluntary arrangement approved on

(c) Insert date

(c)

present overleaf my/our abstract of receipts and payments for the period from

(c)

to

(c)

number of continuation sheets (if any) attached

Signed _____ Date _____

Presentor's name, address and reference (if any)

For Official use

Liquidation Section	Post Room

The Insolvency Act 1986

Form 1.4 (Scot)

Notice of Completion of Voluntary Arrangement

R1.23(3)

Pursuant to Rule 1.23(3) of the Insolvency (Scotland) Rules 1986

To the Registrar of Companies

For official use

Company number

Name of Company

(a) Insert name of company

(a)

(b) Insert full name and address

I (b)

(c) Insert date

the supervisor of a voluntary arrangement approved on
(c) _____ enclose a copy of my notice to the creditors and members of the above-named company that the voluntary arrangement has been completed, together with a copy of my report of my receipts and payments

Signed _____ Date _____

Presentor's name, address and reference (if any)

For Official use

Liquidation Section | Post Room

Rule 2.2

The Insolvency Act 1986

Form 2.1 (Scot)

Notice of Petition for Administration Order

R2.2(1)

Pursuant to section 9(2)(a) of the Insolvency Act 1986 and Rule 2.2(1) of the Insolvency (Scotland) Rules 1986

(a) Insert name of the person to whom notice is to be sent in terms of section 9(2)(a) and Rule 2.2(1)

To (a)

For official use

Company number

Insert name of company

Name of Company

Insert name of person giving notice

I/We _____

of _____

give notice that a petition for an administration order against the above company was presented to the Court on:

Insert date

Signed _____ Date _____

Petitioner/Petitioner's Agent

Presentor's name, address and reference (if any)

For Official use

Insolvency Section | Post Room

103

The Insolvency Act 1986

Notice of Administration Order

Form 2.2 (Scot)

R2.3(3)

Pursuant to section 21(2) of the Insolvency Act 1986 and Rule 2.3(3) of the Insolvency (Scotland) Rules 1986

(a) Insert name of person to whom copy of the order is to be sent in terms of section 21(2) and Rule 2.3(3)

To (a)

For official use

Company number

Insert name of company

Name of Company

Insert name of person giving notice

I/We _____

of _____

_____

_____

_____

give notice that an administration order was made against the above company on:

Insert date

and I/We attach a copy of the administration order certified by the clerk of court.

Signed _____ Date _____

Joint/Administrator(s)

Presentor's name, address and reference (if any)

For Official use

Insolvency Section | Post Room

The Insolvency Act 1986

Notice of Dismissal of Petition for Administration Order

R2.3(4)

Pursuant to Rule 2.3(4) of the Insolvency (Scotland) Rules 1986

* Delete as appropriate

* To the Registrar of Companies

* To the Keeper of the Register of Inhibitions and Adjudications

For official use

Company number

Name of Company

Insert name of company

Insert name of person giving notice

I/We _____

of _____

_____

_____

give notice that on:

Insert date

the petition for an administration order against the company was dismissed. A copy, certified by the clerk of court, of the court's order dismissing the petition is attached.

Signed _____ Date _____
Petitioner/Petitioner's Agent

Presentor's name, address and reference (if any)

For Official use

Insolvency Section | Post Room

The Insolvency Act 1986 Form 2.4 (Scot)

Notice of Discharge of Administration Order

R2.3(4)

Pursuant to sections 18(4) and 24(5) of the Insolvency Act 1986 and Rule 2.3(4) of the Insolvency (Scotland) Rules 1986

To the Registrar of Companies

For official use

Company number

Name of Company

Insert name of company

Insert name of person giving notice

I/We

of

administrator(s) of the company hereby give notice that on:

Insert date

the administration order was discharged. A copy, certified by the clerk of court, of the court's order of discharge is attached.

Signed _____ Date _____

Presentor's name, address and reference (if any)

For Official use

Liquidation Section | Post Room

106

The Insolvency Act 1986

Notice Requiring Submission of Administration Statement of Affairs

Pursuant to section 22(4) of the Insolvency Act 1986 and Rule 2.4(2) of the Insolvency (Scotland) Rules 1986

(a) Insert name of company in administration

(a) _____

(b) Insert full name of administrator

(c) Insert full name of person required to submit statement

(d) Insert date by which statement must be submitted under section 22(4) or (5)

Take note that I, (b) _____

require you (c)_____

to submit a statement as to the affairs of the company by (d)

The statement shall be in the prescribed form of which a copy is attached.

Dated this_____day of _____ 19 _____

Signed _____

Warning

If without reasonable excuse you fail to comply with any obligation under section 22, you will be liable:

(i) On summary conviction to a fine not exceeding the statutory maximum and, for continued contravention, to a daily default fine not exceeding one-tenth of the statutory maximum.

(ii) On conviction on indictment to a fine.

Statement of Affairs

Pursuant to section 22(1) of the Insolvency Act 1986 and Rule 2.5(1) of the Insolvency (Scotland) Rules 1986

Insert name of the company

Statement as to the affairs of

as at the _____ 19__, the date of the administration order

Affidavit

This affidavit must be sworn/affirmed before a Notary Public, Justice of the Peace or Commissioner for Oaths or other person duly authorised to administer the oath, when you have completed the rest of this form.

(a) Insert the name(s) and occupation(s) of deponent(s)

I/We (a) _____

_____

(b) Insert full address(es)

(b) _____

_____

do swear/affirm that the statement set out overleaf and the lists A to G annexed and signed as relative hereto are to the best of my/our knowledge and belief a full true and complete statement as to the affairs of the above named company as at

(c) Insert date of the administration order

(c) _____ the date of the administration order.

Sworn/Affirmed at _____
Date   _____
Signature(s)   _____
Before me   _____
                          Person administering the oath/affirmation

The person administering the oath/affirmation is particularly requested, before swearing or affirming the affidavit, to make sure that the full name, address and description of the Deponent(s) are stated, and to initial any crossings-out or other alterations in the printed form.

STATEMENT as to affairs of the company on the _____

	Estimated Realisable Values £

ASSETS

Assets not specifically secured (as per List "A") _____

Assets specifically secured (as per List "B")	£
Estimated realisable value	
Less: Amount due to secured creditors	
Estimated Surplus _____	

Estimated Total Assets available for preferential creditors,

holders of floating charges and unsecured creditors _____

LIABILITIES

Preferential creditors (as per List "C") _____

Estimated balance of assets available for-

holders of floating charges and unsecured creditors _____

Holders of floating charges (as per List "D") _____

Estimated surplus/deficiency as regards holders of floating charges _____

Unsecured Creditors	£
Trade accounts (as per List "E") _____	
Bills payable (as per List "F") _____	
Contingent or other liabilities (as per List "G") _____	
Total unsecured creditors _____	

Estimated Surplus/Deficiency as regards creditors

Issued and Called-up Capital _____

Estimated Surplus/Deficiency as regards members

These figures must be read subject to the following:—

[(a) There is no unpaid capital liable to be called up]†

[(b) The nominal amount of unpaid capital liable to be called up is £   estimated to

produce £   which is/is not charged in favour of the holder of the Floating Charges]†

The estimates are subject to expenses of the administration and to any surplus or deficiency on trading pending realisation of the Assets.

Page 2

109

Statement of affairs LIST 'A'

Assets not specifically secured

Particulars of assets	Book value £	Estimated to produce £
Balance at bank		
Cash in hand		
Marketable securities (as per schedule I)		
Bills receivable (as per schedule II)		
Trade debtors(as per schedule III)		
Loans and advances (as per schedule IV)		
Unpaid calls (as per schedule V)		
Stock in trade _____		
_____		
_____		
Work in progress _____		
_____		
_____		
Heritable property		
Leasehold property		
Plant, machinery and vehicles		
Furniture and fittings, etc		
Patents, trade marks, etc		
Investments other than marketable securities ...		
Other property		
Total		

Signed

Date

SCHEDULE I TO LIST 'A'

Statement of affairs

Marketable Securities

Names to be arranged in alphabetical order and numbered consecutively

No	Name of organisation in which securities are held	Details of securities held	Book Value £	Estimated to produce £

Signed _____ Date _____

Please do not
write in this
margin

Please complete
legibly, preferably
in black type, or
bold block lettering

SCHEDULE II TO LIST 'A'

Statement of affairs

Bills of exchange, promissory notes, etc, available as assets

Names to be arranged in alphabetical order and numbered consecutively

No	Name and Address of acceptor of bill or note	Amount of bill or note £	Date when due	Estimated to produce £	Particulars of any property held as security for payment of bill or note

Signed _____   Date _____

Please do not
write in this
margin

Please complete
legibly, preferably
in block type, or
bold block lettering

SCHEDULE III TO LIST 'A'

Statement of affairs

Trade debtors

Names to be arranged in alphabetical order and numbered consecutively

No	Name and Address of debtor	Particulars of any securities held for debt	Amount of debt £	Estimated to produce £

Note:

If the debtor to the company is also a creditor, but for a lesser amount than his indebtedness, the gross amount due to the company and the amount of the contra account should be shown in the third column, and only the balance be inserted in the fourth column. No such claim should be included in List 'E'

Signed   Date

113

SCHEDULE IV TO LIST 'A'

Statement of affairs

Loans and Advances

Names to be arranged in alphabetical order and numbered consecutively

No	Name and Address of debtor	Particulars of any securities held for debt	Amount of debt £	Estimated to produce £

Signed _____ Date _____

114

SCHEDULE V TO LIST 'A'

Statement of affairs

Unpaid calls

Names to be arranged in alphabetical order and numbered consecutively

No	No. in share register	Name and Address of shareholder	No. of shares held	Amount of call per share unpaid £	Total amount due £	Estimated to produce £

Signed   Date

Please do not
write in this
margin

Please complete
legibly, preferably
in black type, or
bold block lettering

LIST 'B' (consisting of _____ pages)

Statement of affairs

Assets specifically secured and creditors fully or partly secured (see note below)
(not including debenture holders secured by a floating charge)

No	Particulars of assets specifically secured and nature of security	Date when security granted	Name of creditor	Address and occupation

Note: For this purpose treat as a creditor but identify separately
  (a) an owner of goods in the company's possession under a hire-purchase agreement or an agreement for the hire of goods for more than 3 months, or
  (b) a seller of goods to the company claiming a retention of title or a seller under a conditional sale agreement; — state the nature of the agreement and its date.

116

Please do not
write in this
margin

The names of the secured creditors are to be shownagainst the assets on which their claims are secured, numbered consecutively, and arranged in alphabetical order as far as possible

Please complete
legibly, preferably
in black type, or
bold block lettering

Consideration	Estimated value of assets specifically secured	Total amount due creditor	Balance of debt secured	Balance of debt unsecured carried to List E	Estimated surplus from security
	£	£	£	£	£

Signed _____   Date _____

117

Please do not
write in this
margin

Please complete
legibly, preferably
in black type; or
bold block lettering

LIST 'C' (consisting of _____ pages)

Statement of affairs

Preferential creditors for taxes, salaries, wages and otherwise

Names to be arranged in alphabetical order and numbered consecutively

No	Name of creditor	Address

Please do not
write in this
margin

Please complete
legibly, preferably
in black type, or
bold block lettering

Nature of claim	Total amount of claim	Amount ranking as preferential	Balance not preferential carried to List 'E'

Signed _____   Date _____

119

Please do not
write in this
margin

Please complete
legibly, preferably
in black type, or
bold block lettering

LIST 'D'

Statement of affairs

List of holders of debentures secured by a floating charge

Names to be arranged in alphabetical order and numbered consecutively

No	Name and Address of holder	Amount £	Description of assets over which security extends

Signed _____   Date _____

Statement of affairs

Unsecured creditors — trade accounts. Identify separately on this list customers claiming amounts paid in advance of the supply of goods and services.

Names to be arranged in alphabetical order and numbered consecutively

Please do not write in this margin

Please complete legibly, preferably in black type, or bold block lettering

Note

* When there is a contra account against the creditor less than his claim against the company, the balance only should be inserted under the heading 'Amount of the debt'

No	Name and address of creditor	Amount of the debt * £

Signed   Date

LIST 'F'

Statement of affairs

Unsecured creditors — Bills payable, promissory notes, etc.

Names to be arranged in alphabetical order and numbered consecutively

No	Name and address of acceptor of bill or note	Name and address of holder*	Date when due	Amount of claim £

Signed   Date

LIST 'G'

Statement of affairs

Unsecured creditors — contingent liabilities

Names to be arranged in alphabetical order and numbered consecutively

No	Name and address of creditor	Nature of liability	Amount of claim £

Signed _____   Date _____

Rule 2.7

The Insolvency Act 1986

Notice of Statement of Administrator's Proposals

Pursuant to section 23(1)(a) of the Insolvency Act 1986 and Rule 2.7 of the Insolvency (Scotland) Rules 1986

Form 2.7 (Scot)

S23(1)(a)

To the Registrar of Companies

For official use

Company number

Name of Company

Insert name of company

Insert name of person giving notice

I/We _____

of _____

_____

_____

administrator(s) of the company attach my/our proposals for achieving the purposes set out in the administration order made in relation to above named company on (a) _____. A copy of these proposals was sent to all known creditors on:

(a) Insert date

(a)

and I/we attach a copy of my/our statement to creditors in terms of Rule 2.7.

Signed _____ Date _____

Administrator(s)

Presentor's name, address and reference (if any):

For official use

Insolvency section	Post room

124

The Insolvency Act 1986

Form 2.8 (Scot)

Notice of Result of Meeting of Creditors

Pursuant to section 24(4)/25(6) of the Insolvency Act 1986

**S24(4)/
25(6)**

To the Registrar of Companies

For official use

Company number

Name of Company

Insert name of company

Insert name of person giving notice

I/We _____

of _____

_____

_____

_____

administrator(s) of the company attach a copy of my/our report to the Court dated:

Insert date

detailing the resolution(s) passed at a meeting of creditors held on:

Insert date

Signed _____ Date _____

Administrator(s)

Presentor's name, address and reference (if any)

For Official use

Insolvency Section

Post Room

125

The Insolvency Act 1986

Form 2.9 (Scot)

R2.17

Administrator's Abstract of Receipts and Payments

Pursuant to Rule 2.17(1) of the Insolvency (Scotland) Rules 1986

* Delete as appropriate

* To the Registrar of Companies
* To the Court
* To members of the creditors' committee

For official use

Company number

Name of Company

Insert name of company

Insert name of person giving notice

I/We _____

of _____

administrator(s) of the company present overleaf the abstract of receipts and payments of the company for the period

from

Insert date

to

Insert date

number of continuation sheets (if any) attached

Signed _____ Date _____
        Administrator(s)

Presentor's name, address and reference (if any)

For Official use

Insolvency Section   Post Room

Abstract

Note

The receipts and payments must severally be added up at the foot of each sheet and the totals carried forward from one abstract to another without any intermediate balance so that the gross totals shall represent the total amounts received and paid by the administrator since he was appointed

Receipts	£	p
Brought forward from previous Abstract (if any)		
Carried forward to *Continuation Sheet/next Abstract		

* Delete as appropriate

Payments	£	p
Brought forward from previous Abstract (if any)		
Carried forward to *Continuation Sheet/next Abstract		

* Delete as appropriate

127

Statement of Administrator's Proposed Revisions and Notice of Meeting to Consider Them

Pursuant to section 25(2)(a) of the Insolvency Act 1986

Insert full name of
company   _____

Notice is hereby given that a meeting of creditors of the above named company is to be held
at_____
on the _____ day of _____ 19_____
at_____ to consider revisions of
the proposals which were approved by its creditors on
the _____ day of _____ 19_____

The revisions I/we propose are:

_____
_____
_____

The reasons for these revisions are:

_____
_____
_____

A proxy form is enclosed which should be completed and returned to me by the date of the meeting if you cannot attend the meeting and wish to be represented.

Signed _____
                Administrator(s)

Section 15(7)

The Insolvency Act 1986

Form 2.11 (Scot)

Notice of Order to Deal with Secured Property

S15(7)

Pursuant to section 15(7) of the Insolvency Act 1986

To the Registrar of Companies

| For official use |
| |

Company number

Name of Company

Insert name of company

I/We _____

of _____

Insert name of person giving notice

* Delete whichever is not applicable

administrator(s) of the company obtained an order for the disposal of *secured property/goods in possession of the company under a *hire purchase/conditional sale/hiring/retention of title agreement on

Insert date

A copy of the said Court order certified by the clerk of court is attached.

Signed _____ Date _____
    Administrator(s)

Presentor's name, address and reference (if any):

For official use

Insolvency Section | Post Room

Section 18(4)

The Insolvency Act 1986

Notice of Variation of Administration Order

Pursuant to section 18(4) of the Insolvency Act 1986

To the Registrar of Companies

Form 2.12 (Scot)

S18(4)

For official use

Company number

Name of Company

Insert name of company

Insert name of person giving notice

I/We

of

administrator(s) of the company hereby give notice that on:

Insert date

an order varying the administration order was made. A copy of the said order of variation certified by the clerk of court is attached.

Signed _____ Date _____

Administrator(s)

Presentor's name, address and reference (if any):

For official use

Liquidation Section

Post Room

Notice to Court of Resignation of Administrator

Pursuant to section 19(1) of the Insolvency Act 1986 and Rule 2.18 of the Insolvency (Scotland) Rules 1986

(a) Insert name of the company

(a) _____

(b) Insert full name and address of administrator

I, (b) _____

_____

_____

the administrator of the above company give notice that I am resigning from the said office of administrator

(c) Insert date

with effect from (c) _____

(d) See Rule 2.18

For the following reason(s): (d)_____

_____

_____

_____

Signed _____

Dated _____

(e) The date must be at least 7 days before that stated at (c) above

I confirm that on (e) _____
I gave notice to (f):

(f) See section 13(3) and Rule 2.18

   (i) _____

   (ii) _____

   (iii) _____

being persons who under section 13(3) of the Insolvency Act 1986 are entitled to apply for a vacancy in the office of administrator to be filled.

Notice Requiring Submission of Receivership Statement of Affairs

Pursuant to section 66(1) and (4) of the Insolvency Act 1986 and Rule 3.2(1) of the Insolvency (Scotland) Rules 1986

(a) Insert name of the company in receivership

(a) _____

(b) Insert full name of receiver

(c) Insert full name of person required to submit statement

(d) Insert date by which statement must by submitted under section 66(4) and (5)

Take note that I, (b) _____
require you (c)_____
to submit a statement as to the affairs of the company by
(d)_____

The statement shall be in the prescribed form of which a copy is attached.

Dated this_____day of _____ 19 ____

Signed _____

Warning
If without reasonable excuse you fail to comply with any obligation under section 66, you will be liable:

(i) On summary conviction to a fine not exceeding the statutory maximum and, for continued contravention, to a daily default fine not exceeding one-tenth of the statutory maximum.

(ii) On conviction on indictment to a fine.

Rule 3.9

The Insolvency Act 1986

Form 3.2 (Scot)

Receiver's Abstract of Receipts and Payments

R3.9

Pursuant to Rule 3.9(1) and (3) of the Insolvency (Scotland) Rules 1986

(a) Insert names of persons to whom notice is to be given under Rule 3.9(1)

To (a)

For official use

Company number

Name of Company

Insert name of company

I/We _____

of _____

_____

_____

appointed receiver(s) of the company on

Insert date

present overleaf my/our abstract of receipts and payments for the period from

Insert date

to

Insert date

number of continuation sheets (if any) attached

Signed _____ Date _____

Presentor's name, address and reference (if any)

For Official use

Receivers Section | Post Room

Abstract

Receipts	£	p
Brought forward from previous Abstract (if any)		
Carried forward to *Continuation Sheet/next Abstract		

Payments	£	p
Brought forward from previous Abstract (if any)		
Carried forward to *Continuation Sheet/next Abstract		

The Insolvency Act 1986

Notice of Receiver's Death

Pursuant to Rule 3.10 of the Insolvency (Scotland) Rules 1986

Form 3.3 (Scot)

R3.10

For official use

(a) Insert names of persons to whom notice is to be given under Rule 3.10

To (a)

Company number

Name of Company

Insert name of company

Insert name and address of receiver

receiver of the above company died on:

Insert date

Signed _____ Date _____

Holder of the floating charge or his Agent

Presentor's name, address and reference (if any)

For Official use

Receivers Section | Post Room

Section 61(6)

The Insolvency Act 1986

Form 3.4 (Scot)

Notice of Authorisation to Dispose of Secured Property

S61(6)

Pursuant to section 61(6) of the Insolvency Act 1986

To the Registrar of Companies

For official use

Company number

Insert name of company

Name of Company

Insert names(s) and address(es) of receiver(s)

I/We_____

of _____

_____

_____

receiver(s) of the company obtained an authorisation under section 61(2) of the Insolvency Act 1986 to dispose of property which is subject to a security on

Insert date

A copy of the court's order of authorisation, certified by the clerk of court, is attached.

Signed _____ Date _____

Presentor's name, address and reference (if any)

For Official use

Receivers Section	Post Room

Section 67(1)

The Insolvency Act 1986

Notice of Receiver's Report

Pursuant to section 67(1) of the Insolvency Act 1986

Form 3.5 (Scot)

S67(1)

(a) Insert names of persons to whom notice is to be given under section 67(1)

To (a)

For official use

Company number

Insert name of company

Name of Company

Insert name(s) and address(es) of receiver(s)

I/We _____

of _____

_____

_____

receiver(s) of the company attach a copy of my/our report to creditors and a summary of the statement of affairs of the company.

Signed _____ Date _____

Presentor's name, address and reference (if any)

For Official use

Receivers Section | Post Room

The Insolvency Act 1986   **Form 4.1 (Scot)**

Statutory Demand for Payment of Debt

Pursuant to Section 123(1)(a) or Section 222(1)(a) of the Insolvency Act 1986

Warning

● This is an important document. This demand must be dealt with within 21 days of its service upon the company or a winding up order could be made in respect of the company

● Please read the demand and the notes carefully

● There are additional notes overleaf

Demand

To _____

Address _____

_____

This demand is served by the creditor:

Name _____

Address _____

_____

The creditor claims that the company owes the following debt:

When incurred (1)	Description of debt (2)	Amount due as at the date of this demand (3)
_____	_____	_____
_____	_____	_____
_____	_____	_____
_____	_____	_____
_____	_____	_____

Amount of Debt   £ [   ]

The creditor demands that the company pays the above debt or secures or compounds for it to the creditor's satisfaction

Signature _____

Name _____
         (BLOCK LETTERS)

Position with or relationship to creditor _____

_____ duly authorised

Address _____

_____

Tel. No. _____

Ref. _____

N.B. The person making this demand must complete the whole of this page and Parts A and B on page 2.

Notes for Creditors

● This demand can only be used if the company owes the creditor a sum exceeding £750.

● If the creditor is entitled to the debt by way of assignation, details of the original creditor and any intermediate assignees should be given in Part B on page 2.

● If the amount of debt includes interest, details should be given in column (2), or in a separate note attached to this document, including the grounds upon which interest is charged. The amount of interest must be shown separately in column (3).

● Any other charge payable from time to time may be claimed. The amount or rate of the charge must be identified and the grounds on which it is claimed must be stated.

● In either case the amount claimed must be limited to that which has accrued and is due at the date of the demand.

● If signatory is a solicitor or other agent of the creditor the name of his/her firm should be given.

Part A

The person or persons to whom any communication regarding this demand should be addressed is/are

_____

Address _____

_____

Tel. No. _____

Part B

For completion if the creditor is entitled to the debt by way of assignation

	Name	Date(s) of Assignation
Original creditor		
Assignees		

How to comply with a statutory demand

If the company wishes to avoid a winding-up petition being presented it must pay the debt set out on page 1 of this notice within the period of 21 days of its service upon it. Alternatively, it can attempt to come to a settlement with the creditor. To do this it should:

> inform the person (or one of them, if more than one) named in Part A above immediately that it is willing and able to offer security for the debt to the creditor's satisfaction; or

> inform the person named in Part A immediately that it is willing and able to compound for the debt to the creditor's satisfaction.

If the company disputes the demand in whole or in part or it wishes to come to a settlement it should:

> contact the person named in Part A immediately.

REMEMBER! The company has only 21 days from the date of service on it of this document before the creditor may present a winding-up petition

Section 130

The Insolvency Act 1986

Form 4.2 (Scot)

Notice of Winding up Order

Pursuant to section 130 of the Insolvency Act 1986

S130

To the Registrar of Companies

For official use

Company number

Name of Company

(a) Insert name of company

(a)

(b) Insert full name and address of person giving the notice on behalf of the company

I (b)

(c) Insert date

give notice that on (c) _____ a winding up order was made

(d) Insert name of court

against the above named company by an order of the (d) _____
_____ dated (c) _____

and I attach a copy of the order.

Dated _____

(e) Delete as appropriate

Signed _____
(e) Liquidator/Position in relation to the company

Name(s) in BLOCK LETTERS _____

Presentor's name, address and reference (if any):

For official use

Liquidation Section

Post Room

Notice Requiring Submission of Statement of Affairs

Pursuant to section 131(4) of the Insolvency Act 1986 and Rule 4.7(3) of the Insolvency (Scotland) Rules 1986

(a) Insert name of company in liquidation

(a) _____

(b) Insert full name of liquidator

(c) Insert full name of person required to submit statement

(d) Insert date by which statement must be submitted under section 131(4) or (5)

Take note that I, (b) _____

require you (c)_____

to submit a statement as to the affairs of the company by

(d) _____

The statement must be in the prescribed form, of which a copy is attached, and should give the following further information:

(e) Insert details of any further information required

(e) _____

_____

Dated this_____day of _____ 19 _____

Signed _____

Warning

If without reasonable excuse you fail to comply with any obligation under section 131, you will be liable:

    (i) On summary conviction to a fine not exceeding the statutory maximum and, for continued contravention, to a daily default fine not exceeding one-tenth of the statutory maximum.

    (ii) On conviction on indictment to a fine.

The Insolvency Act 1986   **Form 4.4 (Scot)**

Statement of Affairs

**Pursuant to sections 95, 99 and 131 of the Insolvency Act 1986
and Rules 4.7 and 4.8 of the Insolvency (Scotland) Rules 1986**

Insert name of the
company

Statement as to affairs of

Affidavit

This affidavit must be sworn/affirmed before a Notary Public,
Justice of the Peace or Commissioner for Oaths or other person
duly authorised to administer oaths, when you have completed
the rest of this form.

(a) Insert full
   name(s) and
   occupation(s) of
   deponent(s)

(b) Insert full
   address(es)

I/We (a) _____

_____

of (b) _____

_____

do swear/affirm that the statement set out overleaf and the lists A
to G annexed and signed as relative hereto are to the best of
my/our knowledge and belief a full, true and complete statement
as to the affairs of the above named company as at

(c) insert date of
   commencement
   of the winding up
   which is:
    (i) in a
   voluntary
   winding up the
   date of the
   resolution by the
   company for
   winding up
   (section 86); and
    (ii) in a winding
   up by the court,
   the date of the
   presentation of
   the petition for
   winding up
   unless it is
   preceded by a
   resolution for
   voluntary
   winding up under
   (i) (section 129),
   but in the case of
   a creditors'
   voluntary
   winding up, the
   date inserted
   should be the
   nearest
   practicable date
   before the date
   of the meeting of
   creditors under
   section 98.

(c) _____

Sworn/affirmed at _____

Date _____

Signature(s) of deponent(s) _____

_____

Before me_____
               Person administering the oath or affirmation

**The person administering the oath or affirmation is particularly
requested, before swearing the affidavit, to make sure that the
full name, address and description of the Deponent(s) are stated,
and to ensure that any crossings-out or other alterations in the
printed form are initialled.**

NOTE

This affidavit should be sworn/affirmed and the statement made out and
submitted:
   (1) in a winding up by the court by any person required to do so under
section 131 of the Act by the Liquidator;
   (2) in a members' voluntary winding up which becomes a creditors'
voluntary winding up under sections 95 and 96, by the Liquidator under
section 95; and
   (3) in a creditors' voluntary winding up, by the directors.

STATEMENT as to affairs of the company as at _____

	Estimated Realisable Values £
ASSETS	
Assets not specifically secured (as per List "A") _____	
Assets specifically secured (as per List "B") £	
Estimated realisable value	
Less: Amount due to secured creditors	
Estimated Surplus _____	
Estimated Total Assets available for preferential creditors,	
holders of floating charges and unsecured creditors _____	
LIABILITIES	
Preferential creditors (as per List "C") _____	
Estimated balance of assets available for-	
holders of floating charges and unsecured creditors _____	
Holders of floating charges (as per List "D") _____	
Estimated surplus/deficiency as regards holders of floating charges _____	
Unsecured Creditors £	
Trade accounts (as per List "E") _____	
Bills payable (as per List "F") _____	
Contingent or other liabilities (as per List "G") _____	
Total unsecured creditors _____	
Estimated Surplus/Deficiency as regards creditors	
Issued and Called-up Capital _____	
Estimated Surplus/Deficiency as regards members	

These figures must be read subject to the following:—

    [(a) There is no unpaid capital liable to be called up]†
    [(b) The nominal amount of unpaid capital liable to be called up is £   estimated to
    produce £   which is/is not charged in favour of the holders of Floating Charges]†

    The estimates are subject to expenses of the Liquidation and to any surplus or deficiency on trading pending realisation of the Assets.

Page 2

Please do not write
in this margin

Please complete
legibly, preferably
in black type, or
bold block lettering

Statement of affairs LIST 'A'

Assets not specifically secured

Particulars of assets	Book value £	Estimated to produce £
Balance at bank		
Cash in hand		
Marketable securities (as per schedule I)		
Bills receivable (as per schedule II)		
Trade debtors(as per schedule III)		
Loans and advances (as per schedule IV)		
Unpaid calls (as per schedule V)		
Stock in trade _____ _____ _____		
Work in progress _____ _____ _____		
Heritable property		
Leasehold property		
Plant, machinery and vehicles......................		
Furniture and fittings, etc		
Patents, trade marks, etc		
Investments other than marketable securities		
Other property		
Total		

Signed   Date

144

SCHEDULE I TO LIST 'A'

Statement of affairs

Marketable Securities

Names to be arranged in alphabetical order and numbered consecutively

No	Name of organisation in which securities are held	Details of securities held	Book Value £	Estimated to produce £

Signed _____ Date _____

SCHEDULE II TO LIST 'A'

Statement of affairs

Bills of exchange, promissory notes, etc, available as assets

Names to be arranged in alphabetical order and numbered consecutively

No	Name and Address of acceptor of bill or note	Amount of bill or note £	Date when due	Estimated to produce £	Particulars of any property held as security for payment of bill or note

Signed _____   Date _____

146

Please do not
write in this
margin

Please complete
legibly, preferably
in black type, or
bold block lettering

SCHEDULE III TO LIST 'A'

Statement of affairs

Trade debtors

Names to be arranged in alphabetical order and numbered consecutively

No	Name and Address of debtor	Particulars of any securities held for debt	Amount of debt £	Estimated to produce £

Note:

If the debtor to the company is also a creditor, but for a lesser amount than his indebtedness, the gross amount due to the company and the amount of the contra account should be shown in the third column, and only the balance be inserted in the fourth column. No such claim should be included in List 'E'

Signed _____   Date _____

147

SCHEDULE IV TO LIST 'A'

Statement of affairs

Loans and Advances

Names to be arranged in alphabetical order and numbered consecutively

No	Name and Address of debtor	Particulars of any securities held for debt	Amount of debt £	Estimated to produce £

Signed _____ Date _____

148

Please do not
write in this
margin

Please complete
legibly, preferably
in block type, or
bold block lettering

SCHEDULE V TO LIST 'A'

Statement of affairs

Unpaid calls

Names to be arranged in alphabetical order and numbered consecutively

No	No. in share register	Name and Address of shareholder	No. of shares held	Amount of call per share unpaid £	Total amount due £	Estimated to produce £

Signed _____   Date

Please do not
write in this
margin

LIST 'B' (consisting of _____ pages)

Statement of affairs

Please complete
legibly, preferably
in black type, or
bold block lettering

Assets specifically secured and creditors fully or partly secured
(not including debenture holders secured by a floating charge)

No	Particulars of assets specifically secured	Date when security granted	Name of creditor	Address and occupation

150

The names of the secured creditors are to be shownagainst the assets on which their claims are secured, numbered consecutively, and arranged in alphabetical order as far as possible

Consideration	Estimated value of assets specifically secured	Total amount due creditor	Balance of debt secured	Balance of debt unsecured carried to List E	Estimated surplus from security
	£	£	£	£	£

Signed _____   Date _____

151

LIST 'C' (consisting of _____ pages)

Statement of affairs

Preferential creditors for taxes, salaries, wages and otherwise

Names to be arranged in alphabetical order and numbered consecutively

No	Name of creditor	Address

Please do not
write in this
margin

Please complete
legibly, preferably
in black type, or
bold block lettering

Nature of claim	Total amount of claim	Amount ranking as preferential	Balance not preferential carried to List 'E'

Signed _____ Date _____

LIST 'D'

Statement of affairs

List of holders of debentures secured by a floating charge

Names to be arranged in alphabetical order and numbered consecutively

No	Name and Address of holder	Amount £	Description of assets over which security extends

Signed _____   Date _____

154

Statement of affairs

Unsecured creditors — trade accounts

Identify separately on this list customers claiming amounts paid in advance of the supply of goods and services.

Names to be arranged in alphabetical order and numbered consecutively

No	Name and address of creditor	Amount of the debt * £

Signed _____   Date _____

LIST 'F'

Statement of affairs

Unsecured creditors — Bills payable, promissory notes, etc.

Names to be arranged in alphabetical order and numbered consecutively

No	Name and address of acceptor of bill or note	Name and address of holder*	Date when due	Amount of claim £

Signed _____ Date _____

LIST 'G'

Statement of affairs

Unsecured creditors — contingent liabilities

Names to be arranged in alphabetical order and numbered consecutively

No	Name and address of creditor	Nature of liability	Amount of claim £

Signed _____   Date _____

157

Liquidator's Statement of Receipts and Payments

Pursuant to Section 192 of the Insolvency Act 1986 and Rule 4.11 of the Insolvency (Scotland) Rules 1986

Name of Company _____

Nature of winding up (Delete as appropriate):—

(a) Members' Voluntary   *(b)* Creditors' Voluntary   *(c)* By the Court

Date of commencement of winding-up _____

Date to which last statement, if any, made up _____

Date to which this statement is made up _____

Name and address of liquidator _____

LIQUIDATOR'S STATEMENT OF ACCOUNTS for the period from _____ to _____

RECEIPTS		PAYMENTS	
Nature of Receipts	Amount £	*Nature of payments*	Amount £
Total receipts from last account		Total payments from last account	
Total receipts carried forward		Total payments carried forward	

158

ANALYSIS OF BALANCE

at_____ 19 ___

	£
Total Receipts, per Account	
Total Payments, per Account	
Balance	

Made up as follows:—

		£
1.	Cash in hands of Liquidator	
2.	Balances at Bank:	
	On Current Account	
	On Deposit Receipt	
3.	Investments made by Liquidator	
	Balance as above	

PROGRESS REPORT

		£
A.	Amount of the total estimated assets and liabilities at the date of the commencement of the winding up per Statement of Affairs	Assets—	
		less: Secured Creditors	
		Debenture Holders	
		less: Preferential claims and services	
		Available for Unsecured Creditors	
		Unsecured creditors	

B. Total amount of the capital paid up at the commencement of the winding up.

C. General description and estimated value of:
  (i) any material alterations to the amounts shown in (A) above
  (ii) outstanding unrealised assets.

D. Causes which delay the termination of the winding up.

E. Period within which the Liquidator expects to complete the winding up.

Signature of Liquidator _____

Date _____

NOTES

(1) Where practicable, receipts and payments should be individually listed, but trading and certain other recurring transactions may be suitably grouped or collated if these are numerous.

(2) Contra items such as cash lodged in bank on current account or on deposit receipt or withdrawn therefrom should be excluded from the receipts and payments.

(3) No balance should be shown on the Account. The balance and its analysis should be entered above.

(4) Where there have been no receipts or payments since the last Account, the Liquidator shall give a certificate to that effect.

This form should be completed and sent to the Registrar, Companies Registration Office, 102 George Street, Edinburgh EH2 3DJ, within thirty days after twelve months from the date of commencement of winding up, and at six-monthly intervals thereafter. The final return should be sent immediately the assets have been fully realised and distributed, notwithstanding that six months may not have elapsed since the last return.

The Insolvency Act 1986

Form 4.6 (Scot)

Notice of Liquidator's Statement of Receipts and Payments

S192

Pursuant to section 192 of the Insolvency Act 1986 and Rule 4.11 of the Insolvency (Scotland) Rules 1986

To the Registrar of Companies

For official use

Company number

Name of Company

(a) Insert name of company

(a)

(b) Insert full name(s) and address(es)

I/We (b)

the liquidator(s) of the company attach my/our Statement of Receipts and Payments under section 192 of the Insolvency Act 1986

Signed _____ date _____

Presentor's name, address and reference (if any)

For Official use

Liquidation Section | Post Room

Statement of Claim by Creditor

Pursuant to Rule 4.15(2)(a) of the Insolvency (Scotland) Rules 1986

WARNING

It is a criminal offence

● for a creditor to produce a statement of claim, account, voucher or other evidence which is false, unless he shows that he neither knew nor had reason to believe that it was false; or

● for a director or other officer of the company who knows or becomes aware that it is false to fail to report it to the liquidator within one month of acquiring such knowledge.

On conviction either the creditor or such director or other officer of the company may be liable to a fine and/or imprisonment.

Notes

(a) Insert name of company

(a) _____
_____
_____
_____

(b) Insert name and address of creditor

(b) _____
_____
_____
_____

(c) Insert name and address, if applicable, of authorised person acting on behalf of the creditor

(c) _____
_____
_____
_____

(d) Insert total amount as at the due date (see note (e) below) claimed in respect of all the debts, the particulars of which are set out overleaf.

I submit a claim of *(d)* £_____ in the liquidation of the above company and certify that the particulars of the debt or debts making up that claim, which are set out overleaf, are true, complete and accurate, to the best of my knowledge and belief.

(e) The due date in the case of a company

    (i) which is subject to a voluntary arrangement is the date of a creditors' meeting in the voluntary arrangement;
    (ii) which is in administration is the date of the administration order;
    (iii) which is in receivership is the date of appointment of the receiver; and
    (iv) which is in liquidation is the commencement of the winding up.

The date of commencement of the winding up is

    (i) in a voluntary winding up the date of the resolution by the company for winding up (section 86 or 98); and
    (ii) in a winding up by the court, the date of the presentation of the petition for winding up unless it is preceded by a resolution for voluntary winding up (section 129).

Signed_____
Creditor/person acting on behalf of creditor

Date _____

L

PARTICULARS OF EACH DEBT

Notes

A separate set of particulars should be made out in respect of each debt.

1. Describe briefly the debt, giving details of its nature, the date when it was incurred and when payment became due.

Attach any documentary evidence of the debt, if available.

1. Particulars of debt

2. Insert total amount of the debt, showing separately the amount of principal and any interest which is due on the debt as at the due date (see note (e)). Interest may only be claimed if the creditor is entitled to it. Show separately the V.A.T. on the debt and indicate whether the V.A.T. is being claimed back from H.M. Customs and Excise.

2. Amount of debt

3. Specify and give details of the nature of any security held in respect of the debt including—

(a) the subjects covered and the date when it was given;

(b) the value of the security.

Security is defined in section 248(b) of the Insolvency Act 1986 as meaning "any security (whether heritable or moveable), any floating charge and any right of lien or preference and any right of retention (other than a right of compensation or set off)". For claims in administration procedure security also includes a retention of title agreement, hire purchase agreement, agreement for the hire of goods for more than three months and a conditional sale agreement (see Rules 2.11 and 2.12).

In liquidation only the creditor should state whether he is surrendering or undertakes to surrender his security; the liquidator may at any time after 12 weeks from the date of commencement of the winding up (note (e)) require a creditor to discharge a security or to convey or assign it to him on payment of the value specified by the creditor.

3. Security for debt

4. In calculating the total amount of his claim in a liquidation, a creditor shall deduct the value of any security as estimated by him unless he surrenders it (see note 3). This may apply in administration (see Rule 2.11).

4. Total amount of the debt

162

Rule 4.19   **The Insolvency Act 1986**   **Form 4.8 (Scot)**

Certificate of Appointment of Liquidator

Pursuant to Rule 4.19 of the Insolvency (Scotland) Rules 1986

(a) Insert name of the company

(a) _____

(b) Delete depending upon whether meeting of creditors, contributories or company

(c) Insert date

(d) State full name and address of liquidator(s) and complete as appropriate if more than one person is appointed

* Delete as appropriate

This is to certify that at a meeting of the (b) [creditors]/ [contributories]/[members] of the above named company held on

(c) _____

(d) _____

having provided a written statement that he is/they are* qualified to act as [an]* insolvency practitioner(s) in relation to the above-named company under the provisions of the Insolvency Act 1986 and that he/they* consent(s) so to act, was/were* appointed liquidator(s)* of the company.

The appointment of the liquidator is to be effective from

(c) _____

Date _____

Signed _____
                                   Chairman

Name in BLOCK LETTERS _____

The Insolvency Act 1986

Form 4.9 (Scot)

R4.19

Notice of Appointment of Liquidator

Pursuant to Rules 4.2, 4.18, 4.19 and 4.27 of the Insolvency (Scotland) Rules 1986

To the Registrar of Companies

For official use

(a) Delete except where the liquidator is appointed by a meeting of creditors or contributories

(a) To the Court

Company number

(b) Insert name of company

Name of Company

(b)

(c) Insert full name(s) and address(es)

I/We (c)

(d) Insert date

* Delete whichever does not apply

give notice that on (d) _____ *I/We *was/were appointed liquidator(s) of

(b) _____

by *an order of the court dated (d) _____

or

*a resolution of a meeting of the *creditors/contributories on

(d) _____

(e) Leave in and complete only where liquidator is appointed to succeed a former liquidator

(e) *I/We *was/were appointed to succeed as liquidator

(f) _____

(f) Insert name and address of former liquidator

who *was removed/resigned from office as liquidator on

(d) _____ and who *has/has not been released.

Date _____

Signed _____
(by each liquidator if more than one)

Name in BLOCK LETTERS _____

Presentor's name, address and reference:

For official use

Liquidation Section	Post Room

The Insolvency Act 1986   **Form 4.10 (Scot)**

Certificate of Removal of Liquidator

**Pursuant to sections 171(2) and 172(2) of the Insolvency Act 1986
and Rules 4.24(1) and 4.25(1) of the Insolvency (Scotland) Rules
1986**

(a) Insert name of
the company

(a) _____

I certify that at a meeting of creditors of the above-named
company held on (b) _____

(b) Insert date

(c) Insert full name
and address of
liquidator

it was resolved that (c)_____
_____
_____
_____

be removed from office as liquidator of the above named
company.

* Delete as
applicable

The meeting *[did not pass any resolution against the liquidator
being given his release]/[resolved that the liquidator be not given
his release].

The removal *[and release] of the liquidator is to be effective from
(b)_____

Date _____

Signed _____
            Chairman

Name in BLOCK LETTERS _____

M

Rules 4.24
4.26
4.28A

The Insolvency Act 1986

Form 4.11 (Scot)

Notice of Removal of Liquidator

R4.24

Pursuant to sections 171(2) and 172(2) of the Insolvency Act 1986 and Rules 4.24, 4.26 and 4.28A of the Insolvency (Scotland) Rules 1986

To the Registrar of Companies

For official use

(a) To the Court

Company number

(a) Delete except where, in the case of a winding up by the Court, the liquidator is removed by a meeting of creditors or contributories

(b) Insert name of company

Name of Company

(b)

(c) Insert full name and address

I (c)

(d) Delete as applicable

the (d) [liquidator of the above-named company]/[the chairman of a meeting of the creditors of the above-named company] held on

(e) Insert date

(e) _____ *[attach a certificate of (d) my/the liquidator's removal from office]

(f) Insert when liquidator is removed by the court and delete from *

(f) attach a copy of the order of the court which removed me from office.

I ceased to hold office as liquidator with effect from

(e) _____

Signed _____ Date _____

Presentor's name, address and reference (if any)

For Official use

Liquidation Section

Post Room

166

Application by Liquidator to the Accountant of Court for his Release

Pursuant to section 173(2)(b), (e)(i) and (3), and section 174(4)(b), (d)(i) and (7) of the Insolvency Act 1986 and Rules 4.25 and 4.28A of the Insolvency (Scotland) Rules 1986

(a) Insert name of the company

(a) _____

(b) Insert full name and address of liquidator

I (b)

the liquidator of the above-named company, apply to the Accountant of Court to grant me a certificate of my release as liquidator as a result of

(c) Insert details of circumstances under which you have ceased to act as liquidator

(c)

Date _____

Signed _____
         Liquidator

Name in BLOCK LETTERS _____

The Insolvency Act 1986

Form 4.13 (Scot)

Certificate by the Accountant of Court of Release of Liquidator

Pursuant to section 173(2)(b), (e)(i) and (3), and section 174(4)(b), (d)(i) and (7) of the Insolvency Act 1986 and Rules 4.25(3)(a) and 4.28A of the Insolvency (Scotland) Rules 1986

(a) Insert name of the company

(a) _____

(b) Insert name of Accountant of Court

(c) Insert date

(d) Insert full name and address of liquidator

(e) Insert date of release

I (b) _____ — ,

Accountant of Court, having considered an application dated

(c) _____ by (d) _____

_____

_____

_____

for his release as liquidator of the above-named company, certify that he is released with effect from (e) _____

Signed _____

Accountant of Court, Parliament House, Edinburgh

Dated _____

The Insolvency Act 1986

Form 4.14 (Scot)

R4.25

Certificate of Release of Liquidator

Pursuant to Rules 4.25 and 4.28A of the Insolvency (Scotland) Rules 1986

* Delete as appropriate

* To the Registrar of Companies

(a) Insert other persons to whom notice is to be given

* To (a)

For official use

Company number

Name of Company

(b) Insert name of company

(b)

(c) Insert full name(s) and address(es)

I/We (c)

The *[liquidator of the above-named company]/[the Accountant of Court] attach a certificate of the release of

(d) Insert full name of former liquidator

(d) _____

as liquidator of the above-named company.

Signed _____ Date _____

Presentor's name, address and reference (if any)

For Official use

Liquidation Section | Post Room

Notice to Court of Resignation of Liquidator

Pursuant to section 172(6) of the Insolvency Act 1986 and Rule 4.29 of the Insolvency (Scotland) Rules 1986

(a) Insert name of company

(a) _____

(b) Insert full name and address of liquidator

I, (b)

liquidator of the above-named company report as follows:

My resignation as liquidator was accepted by a meeting of the

(c) Insert date

company's creditors on (c) _____

(d) Delete as applicable

The meeting (d) [did not pass any resolution against my being given my release as liquidator]/[resolved that I should not be given my release as liquidator]

My resignation (d) [and release] is/are to be effective from (c) _____

Date _____

Signed _____
         Liquidator

Name in BLOCK LETTERS _____

Rules 4.28A
4.29
4.30

The Insolvency Act 1986

Notice of Resignation of Liquidator

Form 4.16 (Scot)

S171(5)

Pursuant to sections 171(5) and 172(6) of the Insolvency Act 1986 and Rules 4.28A, 4.29 and 4.30 of the Insolvency (Scotland) Rules 1986

To the Registrar of Companies

For official use

Company number

Name of Company

(a) Insert name of company

(a)

(b) Insert full name(s) and address(es)

I/We (b)

(c) Leave in and complete only for notice under section 171(5) by liquidator in a members' or creditors' voluntary winding up

(c) give notice that I/we resigned from the office of liquidator(s) of the above company on (d) _____

(d) Insert date

(e) attach a copy of my/our notice to the court under section 172(6)

(e) Delete except in winding up by the court

(f) Delete as appropriate (see Rule 4.30)

(f) attach a copy of the order of the court dated (d) _____ granting me/us leave to resign

Signed _____ Date _____

Presentor's name, address and reference (if any)

For Official use

Liquidation Section

Post Room

The Insolvency Act 1986   Form 4.17 (Scot)

Notice of Final Meeting of Creditors

R4.31

Pursuant to sections 171(6) and 172(8) of the Insolvency Act 1986 and Rule 4.31(4) of the Insolvency (Scotland) Rules 1986

For official use

To the Registrar of Companies

To the Court   Company number

Name of Company

(a) Insert name of company

(a) _____

I/We _____

of _____

_____

_____

_____

the liquidator(s) of the above company give notice that the Final General Meeting of creditors under section *94/106/146 of the Insolvency Act *[was held]/[is deemed, in terms of Rule 4.31(5), to have been held]

* Delete whichever does not apply

(b) Insert date

on (b) _____ and I/We attach a copy of the report which was laid before the meeting.

*No quorum was present at the meeting.

*The following resolutions were passed by the meeting:

_____
_____
_____

*I was/was not released as liquidator.

_____

Signed _____ Date _____
_____

Presentor's name, address and reference (if any)

For Official use

Liquidation Section	Post Room

Rule 4.36

The Insolvency Act 1986

Form 4.18 (Scot)

Notice of Death of Liquidator

Pursuant to Rule 4.36 of the Insolvency (Scotland) Rules 1986

R4.36

(a) Insert other persons to whom notice is to be given under rule 4.36

(b) Insert name of company

(c) Insert full name(s) and address(es)

(d) insert full name

(e) Delete as applicable

To the Registrar of Companies

(a)

For official use

Company number

Name of Company

(b)

I/We (c)

give notice that (d)_____

the liquidator of the above-named company has died.

(e) [A copy of the death certificate is attached]/[The date of death was _____].

Signed _____ Date _____

Presentor's name, address and reference (if any)

For Official use

Liquidation Section

Post Room

N

173

The Insolvency Act 1986

Form 4.19 (Scot)

Notice of Vacation of Office by Liquidator

R4.37

Pursuant to Rule 4.37(2) of the Insolvency (Scotland) Rules 1986

To the Registrar of Companies

(a) To the Court

For official use

Company number

(a) Leave in only in winding up by the Court

Name of Company

(b) Insert name of company

(b)

(c) Insert full name and address

I (c)

(d) Insert date

the liquidator of the above-named company give notice that I vacated office as liquidator on (d) _____ on ceasing to be qualified to act as an insolvency practitioner in relation to the company.

Signed _____ Date _____

Presentor's name, address and reference (if any)

For Official use

Liquidation Section | Post Room

The Insolvency Act 1986   **Form 4.20 (Scot)**

Certificate of Constitution of
*Creditors'/Liquidation Committee

* Delete as
appropriate

Pursuant to Rule 4.42, and that Rule as applied by Rules 2.15 and 3.6, of the Insolvency (Scotland) Rules 1986

(a) Insert name of
the company

(a) _____

(b) Insert name

I, (b)

*Liquidator/Receiver/Administrator of the above named company certify that a *Liquidation/Creditors' Committee has been duly constituted and that the membership is as follows:—

(c) Insert details of
members of
committee

(c)

*[This certificate amends the certificate issued by me on

(d) Insert date

(d) _____]

Date _____

Signed _____
                    *Administrator/Receiver/Liquidator

Name in BLOCK LETTERS _____

The Insolvency Act 1986   Form 4.21 (Scot)

Liquidator's Certificate of Continuance of Liquidation Committee

Pursuant to Rule 4.63(1) of the Insolvency (Scotland) Rules 1986

(a) Insert name of the company

(a) _____

(b) Insert name

I/We (b)
the liquidator(s) of the above-named company certify the continuance of the committee established under section 26 of the Insolvency Act 1986.

* Delete as applicable

(c) Insert details of members of committee

The membership of the committee *is/will be as follows:
(c)

*[No meeting of the contributories of the company was summoned].
*[A meeting of the contributories of the company was held on

(d) Insert date

(d) _____ and]
*[no contributories were elected to be members of the committee]
*[the following contributories were elected to be members of the

(e) Insert details of contributories elected to be members

committee: (e)

].

(f) Insert date of previous certificate

*[This certificate amends the certificate issued by me/us on
(f) _____].

Date _____

Signed _____
                Liquidator/s

Name in BLOCK LETTERS _____

Rules 2.15
3.6
4.42
4.63

The Insolvency Act 1986

Form 4.22 (Scot)

R4.42

Notice of Constitution/Continuance of Liquidation/Creditors' Committee

Pursuant to Rules 2.15, 3.6, 4.42(5) and (6) and 4.63(6) and (7) of the Insolvency (Scotland) Rules 1986

To the Registrar of Companies

For official use

Company number

Name of Company

(a) Insert name of company

(a)

(b) Insert full name(s) and address(es)

I/We (b)

* Delete as appropriate

the *liquidator(s)/receiver(s)/administrator(s) of the above named company:

A. attach *[the certificate]/[amended certificate] of *constitution/continuance of the *liquidation/creditors' committee dated

(c) Insert date

(c)

OR

B. give notice of a change in the membership of the *liquidation/creditors' committee and attach a copy of *my/our report dated

(c)

Signed _____ Date _____

Presentor's name, address and reference (if any)

For Official use

Liquidation Section | Post Room

177

The Insolvency Act 1986   Form 4.23 (Scot)

Liquidator's Certificate that Creditors Paid in Full

Pursuant to Rule 4.59(1) of the Insolvency (Scotland) Rules 1986

(a) Insert name of
the company

(a) _____

(b) Insert name of
liquidator

I, (b)

the liquidator of the above-named company, certify that the
creditors of the company have been paid in full, including interest
in accordance with section 189 of the Insolvency Act 1986.

Date _____

Signed _____
                    Liquidator

Name in BLOCK LETTERS _____

178

Rule 4.59

The Insolvency Act 1986

Form 4.24 (Scot)

Notice of Certificate that Creditors Have Been Paid in Full

R4.59

Pursuant to Rule 4.59(2) of the Insolvency (Scotland) Rules 1986

To the Registrar of Companies

For official use

Company number

Name of Company

(a) Insert name of company

(a)

(b) Insert full name(s) and address(es)

I/We (b)

the liquidator(s) of the above-named company attach a copy of my/our certificate that the creditors of the above-named company have been paid in full with interest.

Signed _____ Date _____

Presentor's name, address and reference (if any)

For Official use

Liquidation Section | Post Room

179

Section 89(3)   **The Insolvency Act 1986**   Form 4.25 (Scot)

Declaration of Solvency   # S89(3)

Pursuant to section 89(3) of the Insolvency Act 1986

To the Registrar of Companies

For official use

Company number

Name of Company

(a) Insert name of
company

(a)

(b) Insert full
name(s) and
address(es)

I/We (b)

attach a declaration of solvency embodying a statement of assets
and liabilities.

Signed _____ Date _____

Presentor's name,
address and
reference (if any)

For Official use

Liquidation Section   Post Room

The Insolvency Act 1986

Declaration of Solvency Embodying a Statement of Assets and Liabilities

Company Number _____

Insert name of the company

Name of Company_____

_____

Presented by _____

Declaration of Solvency

(a) Insert name(s) and address(es)

We (a) _____

_____

_____

_____

(b) Delete as applicable

being (b) [all the]/[the majority of the] directors of (c) _____

(c) Insert name of company

_____

do solemnly and sincerely declare that we have made a full enquiry into the affairs of this company, and that, having done so, we have formed the opinion that this company will be able to pay

(d) Insert a period of months not exceeding 12

its debts in full together with interest at the official rate within a period of (d) _____ months, from the commencement of the winding-up.

We append a statement of the company's assets and liabilities as

(e) Insert date

at (e) _____ being the latest practicable date before the making of this declaration.

We make this solemn declaration, conscientiously believing it to be true, and by virtue of the provisions of the Statutory Declarations Act 1835.

Declared at _____ the _____ day

of _____

before me,

_____

_____

_____

_____
Notary Public, Justice of the Peace or Commissioner for Oaths

_____
Signature(s) of person(s) making declaration

Statement as at _____ showing assets at estimated realisable values
and liabilities expected to rank:

ASSETS AND LIABILITIES	Estimated to realise or to rank for payment to nearest £
ASSETS	£
Balance at Bank	
Cash in Hand	
Marketable Securities	
Bills Receivable	
Trade Debtors	
Loans and Advances	
Unpaid Calls	
Stock in Trade	
Work in Progress	
Heritable Property	
Leasehold Property	
Plant and Machinery	
Furniture, Fittings, Utensils, etc	
Patents, Trade Marks, etc	
Investments other than Marketable Securities	
Other Property, viz	
Estimated Realisable Value of Assets ... ... £	
LIABILITIES	£
Secured on specific assets, viz	
Secured by a Floating Charge(s)	
Estimated Expenses of Liquidation and other expenses including interest accruing until payment of debts in full	

Unsecured Creditors (amounts estimated to rank for payment)

	£	£
Trade Accounts		
Bills payable		
Accrued Expenses		
Other Liabilities		
Contingent Liabilities		

Estimated Surplus after paying Debts in full	£	

Remarks:

The Insolvency Act 1986

Return of Final Meeting in a Voluntary Winding Up

Pursuant to sections 94 and 106 of the Insolvency Act 1986

Form 4.26 (Scot)

S94/
106

For official use

To the Registrar of Companies

Company number

Name of Company

(a) Insert name of company

(a)

(b) Insert full name(s) and address(es)

I/We (b)

give notice:

* Delete as applicable

(c) Insert date

(d) The copy account must be authenticated by the written signature(s) of the liquidator(s)

1. that a general meeting of the company was duly *[held on]/[summoned for] (c) _____ pursuant to Section *[94]/[106] of the Insolvency Act 1986, for the purpose of having an account (of which a copy is attached (d)) laid before it showing how the winding-up of the company has been disposed of and *[that the same was done accordingly]/[no quorum was present at the meeting].

(e) Delete in members' voluntary winding up

(e) 2. that a meeting of the creditors of the company was duly *[held on]/[summoned for] (c) _____ pursuant to section 106 for the purpose of having the said account laid before it showing how the winding up of the company has been conducted and the property of the company has been disposed of and *[that the same was done accordingly]/[no quorum was present at the meeting].

Signed _____ Date _____

Presentor's name, address and reference (if any)

For Official use

Liquidation Section

Post Room

183

Liquidator's Statement of Account in a Voluntary Winding Up

Statement showing how winding up has been conducted and the property of the company has been disposed of.

Name of Company_____

From _____ (commencement of winding up) to _____ (close of winding up)

	Statement of assets and liabilities	Receipts		Payments
Receipts				£
Cash at Bank			Expenses of Solicitors to Liquidator	
Cash in hand			Other Legal Expenses	
Marketable Securities				
Sundry Debtors			Liquidator's Remuneration	
Stock in Trade				
Work in Progress			By whom fixed_____	
Heritable Property				
Leasehold Property				
Plant and machinery			Auctioneer's and Valuer's Charges	
Furniture, Fittings, Utensils, etc			Expenses of Management and Maintenance of Assets of the Company	
Patents, Trademarks, etc			Expenses of Notices in Gazette and Local Paper	
Investments other than Marketable Securities			Incidental Outlays	
Surplus from securities				
Unpaid Calls at Commencement of Winding Up			Total Expenses and Outlays £	
Amount Received from Calls on Members/Contributories made in the Winding Up			(i) Debenture Holders: £	
Receipts per Trading Account			Payment of £ per £ debenture	
Other Property, viz:			Payment of £ per £ debenture	
			Payment of £ per £ debenture	
£			(ii) Creditors: £	
	£		*Preferential	
Less			*Unsecured	
			Dividends of p in £ on £	
Payments to Redeem Securities			(The estimate of amount expected to rank for dividend was £)	
Expenses of Diligence				
Payments per Trading Account			(iii) Returns to Contributories: £	
			.... per £	
			.... † share	
Net realisations £			...... per £	
			.... † share	
			.... per £	
			.... † share	
Note				
* State number. Preferential creditors need not be separately shown if all creditors have been paid in full.			**Balance**	
† State nominal volume and class of share.			£	

(1) Assets, including _____ shown in the statement of assets and liabilities and estimated to be of the value of £_____ have proved to be unreliable.

_____

(2) State amount in respect of:

    (a) unclaimed dividends payable to creditors in the winding up.   £

    (b) other unclaimed dividends in the winding up.   £

    (c) moneys held by the company in respect of dividends or other sums due before the commencement of the winding up to any person as a member of the company.   £

(3) Add here any special remarks the Liquidators think desirable:

Dated_____

Signed (by the Liquidator(s) _____

Names and addresses of Liquidators (IN BLOCK LETTERS) _____

_____

_____

_____

The Insolvency Act 1986

Form 4.27 (Scot)

Notice of Court's Order Sisting Proceedings in Winding Up by the Court

S112/ 147

Pursuant to sections 112(3) and 147(3) of the Insolvency Act 1986

To the Registrar of Companies

For official use

Company number

Name of Company

(a) Insert name of company

(a)

(b) Insert full name and address of person giving notice on behalf of the company

I (b)

(c) Insert date

give notice that on (c) _____ the (d) _____

(d) Insert name of court

made an order sisting the proceedings in the winding up of the above company and I enclose a copy of the order.

Dated _____

Signed _____

(e) Delete as appropriate

(e) Liquidator/Position in Relation to Company

Name in BLOCK LETTERS _____

Presentor's name, address and reference (if any):

For official use

Liquidation Section

Post Room

186

Rule 4.77

The Insolvency Act 1986

Form 4.28 (Scot)

Notice under Section 204(6) or 205(6)

R4.77

Pursuant to section 204(6) or 205(6) of the Insolvency Act 1986 and Rule 4.77 of the Insolvency (Scotland) Rules 1986

To the Registrar of Companies

For official use

Company number

Name of Company

(a) Insert name of company

(a)

(b) Insert full name(s) and address(es)

I/We (b)

(c) Insert full name of court

attach a copy of the order made by the (c) _____
_____dated _____

(d) Delete as applicable

under section (d) [204(5)]/[205(5)] of the Insolvency Act 1986.

Signed _____ Date _____

Presentor's name, address and reference (if any)

For Official use

Liquidation Section

Post Room

EXPLANATORY NOTE

(This Note does not form part of the Rules.)

These Rules set out the detailed procedure for the conduct of insolvency proceedings under the Insolvency Act 1986 ("the Act") relating to companies registered in Scotland and other companies which the Scottish courts have jurisdiction to wind up and otherwise give effect to that Act in relation to Scotland.

Part 1 of the Rules sets out the procedure relating to company voluntary arrangements under Part I of the Act.

Part 2 of the Rules sets out the procedure relating to the administration procedure in Part II of the Act (Administration Orders).

Part 3 of the Rules sets out the procedure relating to receivers in Chapter II of Part III of the Act (Receivers (Scotland)). In addition, the Receivers (Scotland) Regulations 1986 (S.I. 1986/1917) prescribe matters which expressly fall to be prescribed in terms of that Chapter.

Parts 4-6 of the Rules set out the procedure relating to winding up of companies in Part IV of the Act. Part 4 of the Rules deals with winding up by the court. Parts 5 and 6 of, and Schedules 1 and 2 to, the Rules apply the provisions of Part 4, with modifications, to creditors' voluntary winding up and members' voluntary winding up respectively.

Part 7 of the Rules contains provisions of general application to insolvency proceedings. They include provisions relating to meetings (Chapter 1), proxies and company representation (Chapter 2) and miscellaneous matters (Chapter 3). In particular, Schedule 5 contains the forms which are to be used for the purposes of the provisions of the Act or the Rules which are referred to in those forms.

The Rules come into force on 29th December 1986 when the Act comes into force and will apply to insolvency proceedings which are commenced on or after that day.

Printed in the United Kingdom for HMSO
800 WO 1451 C6 6/93 51.0.0 56219 ON 251728